Books by John Greening

**Poetry**
WESTERNERS
WINTER JOURNEYS
THE TUTANKHAMUN VARIATIONS
FOTHERINGHAY AND OTHER POEMS
THE COASTAL PATH
THE BOCASE STONE
NIGHTFLIGHTS: NEW AND SELECTED POEMS
GASCOIGNE'S EGG
OMM SETY
THE HOME KEY
ICELAND SPAR

**Criticism**
POETS OF THE FIRST WORLD WAR
THE POETRY OF W.B. YEATS
FOCUS ON THE POETRY OF TED HUGHES
FOCUS ON THOMAS HARDY, POEMS 1912–13
FOCUS ON EDWARD THOMAS

# HUNTS

# HUNTS
## Poems 1979–2009

JOHN GREENING

GE

**GREENWICH EXCHANGE
LONDON**

**Greenwich Exchange, London**

Hunts, Poems 1979–2009
© John Greening

First published in Great Britain in 2009
All rights reserved

Printed and bound by imprintdigital.net
Typesetting and layout by Jude Keen, London
Tel: 020 8355 4541
Cover design by December Publications, Belfast
Tel: 028 90286559
Cover image: *Flight* © Carry Akroyd

Set in Minion 10/12

Greenwich Exchange Website: www.greenex.co.uk

Cataloguing in Publication Data is available from the
British Library

ISBN: 978-1-906075-33-0

*for Jane, Katie and Rosie*

# ACKNOWLEDGEMENTS

MOST OF THE POEMS in this collection have been selected from the following books and the author gratefully acknowledges their publishers: *Westerners* (Hippopotamus Press, 1982), *Winter Journeys* (Rivelin Press, 1984), *The Tutankhamun Variations* (Bloodaxe Books, 1991), *Fotheringhay and Other Poems* (Rockingham Press, 1995), *The Coastal Path* (Headland Publications, 1996), *The Bocase Stone* (The Dedalus Press, Ireland, 1996), *Nightflights* (Rockingham Press, 1998), *Gascoigne's Egg* (Cargo Press, 2000) *Omm Sety* (Shoestring Press, 2001), *The Home Key* (Shoestring Press, 2003).

Other uncollected poems have appeared in the following publications: *Agenda, Critical Quarterly, Critical Survey, The Dark Horse, Egyptian Bulletin, Interpreter's House, Light Unlocked (Enitharmon), Leviathan, London Magazine, Metre, Other Poetry, Outposts, Poetry Ireland Review, Poetry Review, Poetry Wales, Poets of the First World War, Quadrant (Australia), The Rialto, Seam, Stand, Staple, Swansea Review, Times Literary Supplement.*

Particular thanks for the encouragement of Stuart Henson and Dennis O'Driscoll, who work different vineyards, but share the vintage.

# CONTENTS

# THE WINTER JOURNEY
(1979–1981)

## THE WINTER JOURNEY

*In 1911, three members of Captain Scott's polar expedition (Apsley Cherry-Garrard, Edward ('Bill') Wilson, and 'Birdie' Bowers) undertook a 36-day journey through the dark of an Antarctic winter to collect specimens of the Emperor Penguin's egg. This sequence of 36 sonnets is based on their story.*

1

Tonight the sun turns. It's Christmas. It's Easter.
It's a summer seaside holiday – on ice! In the distance,
the tide crack groaning. But in here, it's roast
pemmican and party games – a 'magnificent bust!'
Birdie's donned a funny hat. Bill has an egg
Cherry's opened for the riddle. Through thick specs
he reads it: *Why is the Emperor Penguin
like the Kaiser?* Outside, the ice cracks.
*Because* – and Titus pops his toy gun,
Evans does the Lancers, and once again our glasses
are filled for a Coronation toast. *Because the one* –
(Even Scott smiles, moonlight on a concealed crevasse)
*Because the one won't take his colonies off the ice,
And the other won't take his eyes off our* – Laughter! Laughter!
                              And the laughter dies.

2

With the Somme yet to leap out from its dark ditch, the lanes
of England throng with youngsters eager to volunteer
and confront horrific odds; and they'll be sure to be cheered
all the way to their catastrophe. But this will not explain
why three such thoughtful and supremely sane
volunteers as Wilson, Bowers and Cherry-Garrard
should be off this winter on an egg hunt, prepared
for anything, with little hope of luck, and none of gain.
It's as if they knew Scott's Message to the Public, 'That Englishmen
can endure hardships, help one another, and meet death
with as great a fortitude as ever in the past',
as if to superimpose that text above their frozen fingers
in a dramatic poster that will probe the faith
of would-be heroes more deeply even than Kitchener's thrust.

3

Wilson: perhaps a virtuoso romantic,
mauve, milk-voiced. The bowed and crystalline
Antarctic was the grand he performed to. Perhaps a saint.
He had a disgust of all impurity. Bill would go to the Pole.
Bowers: short, broad, the plain man, penguin-faced,
whom the exhaustion, the fear, the misery of frost
seldom bit – he'd be at the log still, pony-tending, making some list.
He said that Christ had once appeared to him.
                                   Birdie would go to the Pole.
Cherry-Garrard: a good hard worker, and a perfect brick,
from a distinguished house. Well-heeled and well-liked.
The prose tragedian of the final expedition.
He – perhaps he was too short-sighted – would not be going to the Pole,
but would survive the two world wars, and trace his
own way back, repeatedly, to find those friends' cold faces.

4

The Barrier, and soft snow. We can hardly budge
the sledge-runners. Hard crystal. Could be the Golden
Mile for all the progress after we've hauled
the two loads back and forth along the Barrier edge.
Too much oil, too much equipment! Then you've pulled
off your fur glove to get a firm grasp. What you haven't
yet grasped is that it's minus forty-seven
where your fingers are. But when you come to hold
your supper-dish … Oh for that plain boiled
snow, or tea perhaps, and a Huntley and Palmer's
Emergency Biscuit! The three of us curled
around our cups, we almost think nothing can harm us,
that we will be able to survive that soul-
destroying howl, this cage, the megaton cold.

5

You sweat it. You weep it. You excrete it.
You walk on it. You sleep in it. You eat it.
If you like, you can shake it out, or chuck some heat at it,
but there's still more creeping at your feet.
It's something you learn to live with, ice. To meet it
halfway. The only time you will escape it
is at night, when it thaws, when you're asleep.
So long as you're sleeping it will relax that grip.
But you can never sleep, because of the frost,
because of the fear you won't wake,
because, like the princess, once you rest
you can't be roused. Only if you're kissed.
But all the kings' sons are either stuck fast
or outside still hoping the barrier will break.


6

A six-stone, four-foot bird that never sings,
that swims like a porpoise and dresses
like an impresario; whose prehistoric predecessors
had scaly claws, himself waving feathered wings
he's never been known to use … that's the one
we're here to collect: the Antarctic Emperor.
It lays its eggs on bare ice just in the windiest corner
as the winter sets in. Everyone else has gone,
except this foolhardy creature. And the egg
it enthrones between its belly and its feet,
Bill assures us, is packed with scientific meat,
so it's well worth this few weeks' slog –
difficult though it makes it to distinguish
the Emperors' foolhardiness from that of the English.

7

Ambassadors of 'the Empire on which the sun
etcetera' where the sun won't even rise.
There were stars. We had the moon. The aurora
at times. But most, the wind cracked its blunder-
buss of blizzards, and knocked all the lights
out of the sky. It was the darkness, more
than the cold. Bill's *Time to get up!* Birdie's groan.
Cherry trying to get some use out of his eyes.
When we were bumping through the lower slopes of Terror,
our heels bruised by the sledges as we sped down
into the complete black, once the cloud broke, and the sky
signalled three steps ahead with an ice-mirror.
It flashed about a crevasse. We'd been shown
the trap this time. Perhaps we were not alone.


8

AM GOING SOUTH  AMUNDSEN   What if he tried?
We think of Scott and all the others wintering at the Base.
(Shall we go on? *Yes, yes!* they replied.)
Whether or not we do go, he must decide:
if Scott decides we don't go, England loses face.
AM GOING SOUTH  AMUNDSEN   Would he have lied?
And back home, commiseration, criticism, wide
publicity for our abandoned mission, failure, disgrace ...
(Shall we go on? *Yes, yes!* they replied.)
But if we went we'd have the ranks of England's pride
to defend us – if we went, and if we won that race ...
AM GOING SOUTH  AMUNDSEN   What if he tried?
(Shall we go on? *Yes, yes!* they replied.)
If we don't go we'll wish we had gone even though we died.

9

To howl. A fit of shivering. Your flame gutters.
At a hundred and ten degrees of frost you feel
each fresh drop as a fresh turn on the wheel
of the rack. Like lock-jaw, your body chatters
till a dream has at last solidified: of your mother's
arms and of Papa's bookcase, of cook's hot meals,
of a girl, of girls –
                              But now the Killer Whale's
black nose has broken the floe. It scatters
the fantasy. To howl! It's the ice has seized
you through your bag, has snatched the dream
you hugged between your belly and your feet
and smashed it. Left you, a foetus, to freeze.
Cherry yawns. Birdie snores. And Bill calls *Time* –
To howl? To die? To get up and eat.

10

A blindfold and a flash of white and you drop
down down down (oh dear I shall be late) a jerk!
Stiff. You must be dead. My watch, where – ? I expect
that pink-eyed white angora rabbit hopping
away along the blue glazed corridor there … *All right?*
There's a jar marked 'orange marmalade', I'll just –
*I said are you all right?* Fine, but first I must
just taste this – did you see it? The white – the white …
The crevasse is dark and deep. You can't express
the pressure of your confused faults, only hang stiff
like the hanged man. There is no handhold
word, only the rope. You are within the question
which has no answer. You must let them lift
you, curiouser and curiouser, back up to the blindfold.

11

They swing, they sway, silk curtaining, they flash like swords
or searchlights, lemon, orange, green,
whirling in the east. We lay back our heads
and gazed. Exhausted. Incapable of words.
Wagner. Drury Lane. The kinema. An underground train's
electric flash. Incandescent flickering leads
opening through the dark. Distant power lines
at minus fifty. Ice-angels dancing. Will-o'-the-waste
luring us. The ghosts of the other dead explorers.
We gazed. We were transfixed. Except near-sighted
Cherry, whose lenses were so utterly iced
up he missed the show. *But wasn't it so boring*
*stuck out there? Deprived of everything Society*
*can offer? The bright lights? Didn't you get depressed?*

12

Not a snow petrel. Not an albatross or skua.
Nothing in the bare sky ahead but frost. Might there
perhaps be a penguin? Or are we the three sole survivors of a war.
Something out of Wells. On Mars. Or in somebody else's nightmare.
At home, in the warm, what's a friend?
Someone to drink with, to joke with. On this trek,
that privilege is all you have between your mind
and the ice. He is the Emperor. You are his egg.
If one of us had faltered, he could have cracked
the rest of us. So there was no argument. At worst,
'we reached bedrock' and crawled into our bags
with a dull groan. The weather was all we cursed.
Then laughter. Songs. Obscure faith. And selflessness.
Bill. Birdie. Cherry. Words could not express …

13

Just how utterly exhausted we were,
until we brought the second sledge when our own prints
came to seem like humps we had to lift
each foot across. Even the *Winterreise*
tunes freeze, but feet can't stop. Your harnesses
are bar-lines. The blizzard plays you on.
And though your lips are solid, and your heartbeat's
too slow, you sing, anything, but it must get you there.
*Ein Licht tanzt freundlich* before me.
I'll follow, even though it wants to lure me
to the graveyard with Schubert and Wilhelm Müller.
When you're musically hollow, you surrender yourself
to any gaudy beat. *Hinter Eis und Nacht und Graus*
there is a *helles, warmes Haus.* All I desire is delusion.


14

Antarctica House, its windows are whirls
of bleariness, its furniture is draped white,
the rooms one long chill draught of dark
closed doors. Occasionally, a sheet unfurls
a stony sheen, or the leads in the tracery light
with a stained aurora, only to sink back to the stark
domain of silverware, cut glass, and engraved
mirrors huge as mountain corries. All the clocks
have stopped, their rotating suns permanently down.
All the beds, though invitingly smoothed,
are cold, unoccupied. And each of the household nooks,
that flaw with a spider, a beetle, or a mouse ...
Even the servants have gone. Then who was it passed
us in the butler's pantry, that tail-coated ghost?

15

Tea from wickerwork in a Mallows or a Mawson garden.
With the ladies in Brighton luxury or on a Bexhill beach.
Under the Sunningdale pines in a deevie Ford T,
with golf-clubs. On two wheels strumming a ukelele.
Out at a hop. Or at Hove, watching Alletson's
brief heatwave. On rollerskates down the prom. And at dusk,
magic lanterns, moonlit menus, Gipsy Love, the Machiche, the Galop,
or a dip, with the ladies. The love beneath the stars. The leaving cards.
Smell of melting wax and strawberries, sound
of champagne and Caruso. Punt-pole sticking. Straw hat
floats down to Parson's Pleasure, with the ladies,
mauve and green in the prolonged light, *Che gelida manina*:
that divine, liberty-steeped, easy, golden July
nineteen-eleven. This rigor. This winter of a July of nineteen-eleven.

16

When Houdini challenges them to bind him head to foot,
fetter him, snap handcuffs on him under six stout locks,
then have him screwed into, riveted into a plate-glass box
filled with water, which is then itself closed in; or put
into a strait-jacket, wrapped in thick canvas with straps
of hide and steel buckles, and requests to be hung upside down
from a crane off the top floor of the highest block in town
so he can demonstrate again the ingenuity of his escapes …
there seems to be little to distinguish us. We volunteered
to be thrown into this dark. Asked to be snow-stocked, frost-
manacled, strapped in harnesses, immobilised.
We chose to battle against the clock for dear life, just to be cheered
and called a hero. And we, like Houdini, boasted
we could escape even frozen in a solid block of ice.

17

There is nothing I would not give to be free of this cold,
no sin I would not commit if only I could slip this dark.
Take the next five years! But let it slam, this cold,
behind you. Let me enter your warm oblivion, be safely dead.
My hands, if I could move them, would slash God's cold
and willingly sink towards that fire. And if these wet coils of dark
relaxed and let my eyes see an exit, I'd forsake the angel of cold
and descend rejoicing to the everlasting burning of the dead.
The surface crush. The sastrugi crunch. Your breath's cold
crackle. No landmark. Noise only and the unending dark.
Dreams of skipping through a beech grove. Fantasies that the cold
is really heat and the hollow is alive with the dead.
Weak, wondering why we still go on, so almost dead,
with, what's the point, so almost, going on, so almost dead.


18

Three winters one long winter, more hideous
and harrowing than ever man faced. Feet-thick
the ice, where waves, where a waterfall beat quick
life before. Minute fangs nip your skin, insidious
white devils. As for warmth, to divide the winters,
none till Ragnarok: the sky then will be scorched
as Fenrir, in the east, in Ironwood, watches
the chains be chewed loose and his wolf-monsters
fall upon the world – the summer world, the world
of warmth and women – watches them pulverise it
to a permafrost world, of the wind, of the wolf.
Three winters. The first war in the world
I well remember. The sun gone black, an uncle sacrifices
a nephew, a brother his brother, myself myself.

19

Snowed up, 'snow on snow', we sing. Christina's
bleak winter can't have been a patch on ours.
If she could only have seen these
Three Foolish Men looking for their Emperor's
nesting place, she might have framed a more
sardonic sketch of faith: a penguin
messiah, a pilgrimage to the Source
of Ornithology, a flock of British bedouin
following a star called Scott, sanguine,
single file, in furs and silver, carrying instruments,
formaldehyde, and a box to put the eggs in.
The frosty wind made a moan like innocence
in agony, and the Selfridges display pane
was shattered by a jag of terminal moraine.


20

Hammer the bag's fur mouth open, enter for
your seven-hour stretch on the shark's teeth.
Immortal bird, we've had our beaker full
of the South! Now for a Waterford decanter
and a tulip glass; moist lips, blushes, breath
of cinnamon and cloves; mulled metaphor …
I've seen Mount Erebus scrawl hot smoke
in the ice – and though my pencil lead will freeze
before it can write the equivalent word, sex
is at the core, and almost sufficient. A yogi,
perhaps, could withstand conditions bad as these
by imagining a fire in his solar-plexus,
but we, poor Englishmen, with our endlessly damp fusees,
haven't the spirit, haven't the will for mystic vestas.

21

To create a home must rank, after sex,
as the most insistent urge. The rite
of wall-building. To invoke a finite
motif from the harsh atmospherics
of atonality, where even your own tracks
make no development or resolution. We chose a site
just below the top of the hill, and that same night
attacked the ice. But even with steel picks
evolution from the Glacial to the Palaeolithic takes
more time than you'd imagine. By hurricane light
we lug boulders, shovel snow, and chip white
occasional glimpses of home in igloo blocks.
In such an artificial chromatic glow, these might
well be Cheltenham, Lamer House, HMS Fox.


22

This was the dream, three nights:
one summer
a cold wave had come
and froze the earth to ice.
By the second, Lorraine's
canals were rigid,
that ruddy-faced wine region
white, still. It came
to the third dream. Cold
would have killed
all life – but there was a peach tree
with peach-halves in syrup, which I
reached out to take
and crunched my tongue awake.

23

'The Emperor of the Sorrowful Realm was there:
out of the encircling ice he stood breast high'
and we stand, drugged by the wind's jab, staring
at the wingless bird that flaps as if to fly,
or as if to whip what stuns us on our exposed ledge.
A monster: many-faced, multiple-eyed
Emperor of Hell. Each mouth clenched on the legs
of a sinner. Three at a time. With a piteous sound.
But they are penguins. And we are here for their eggs.
Slither down. Among the addled scraps are found
three whole shells. Into our mitts
and escape back up the mountain. Looking round,
thinking to see the head of the Great Lord of Dis,
we saw only those great broken eggs on the ice.

24

Having descended to where, like at the funeral
of Tolstoy, black pathetic mourners in stiff
procession wound slowly beneath the cliff
supporting their precious charge: Imperial
Penguins' eggs; having snatched enough material
for Bill and the BM (something to show
for it all) plus fuel for the blubber stove,
tonight we ate fresh Emperor! A fitting memorial.
Now all at once we're listening. Some kind of incorporeal
revenge has begun, starting with a deathly calm.
We are being inspected. A million little crabby claws
are preparing to devour us. Inside, the cheery old
atmosphere remains. But outside, the silence has become
unsustainable. It breathes. It scratches at the door.

25

Our hair must be turning white, our mouths
are already toothless. Do our heads tilt
on their axes? Magnetic South, True South,
which? Just wildly spinning? Did the jolt
unbalance us when we fell from our prams?
Does that explain the indulgent smile whenever friends
rebuke: you children think your games
in Never-Never-Land will never end?
Near Kirriemuir I first put my plea
to Bill, persuaded him, near Kirriemuir,
to take me to the Pole. Then, the plot
of the Lost Boys, the Captain, and Peter,
wasn't in our minds. ('My dear Barrie, we are
pegging out in a very comfortless spot …')


26

When, with your compartment windows down, on a holiday
excursion to the coast, you've at last begun to relax
and dissolve with the twin sister giggling of the tracks,
the horses and hills, ploughmen and spires, your express hurls
you all, with two short howls, into a hurricane
of steam, dumb-smothering you with shrieks
of grease and wind, wild hysterics,
and a pandemoniacal dark … It was the same
when we were hit, quite unprepared: *Bill! Bill!* –
like an alarm cord pulled – *the tent has gone!*
sent us staggering madly into the storm.
We fought. We clawed. We dragged what gear was still
left out there into our hut. The tent had gone.
The roof next. And finally any hope of our ever getting warm.

27

Our tent. No sooner reappeared than it has become
The Big Top, and we are the trio billed
to tread the high wire, to perform
above the white wards dim with thrilled
white faces. *Ladies and Gentlemen ...*
Don't you feel the ice-fall nudge you off balance?
Steady your mind now. Grip the mental mean
that sways on either side of you across the silence.
This pole, those flurrying eyes, the dark circus
must go on, in spite of nerves. The nation's
hush has already volunteered your carcass
for the Great hobbling Push towards an ovation.
*Ladies and Gentlemen, from Darkest
Antarctica, the Death-Defying Sensation –*


28

For all that optimistic badinage
when we were lashing down crate after crate of provisions,
pony fodder, and petrol for the motor sledges ...
whenever we stopped, our eyes would move to the horizon
in the south, to that fading, defiant image
in gold, like a sovereign whose head attrition
has reduced to a robe and crown. In an earlier age
one might have even shivered, but the present
is aware that Halley's comet passes on average
once in every lifetime. In nineteen-ten it came. It isn't
expected again till eighty-six. It's not a sign. It doesn't presage.
It simply passes. A wanderer. An icy remainder of fission
in the farthest circle. Yet it set us on edge
to be seeing it there, and sailing in its direction.

29

'Steadfastly, surely,' said the *Express* correspondent,
its twenty thousand tons of nothing slid
'like some movement of Fate ... as a glacier glides
to the sea' ... Steel bauble, diversion for the affluent,
a jerry-built toy. From the White Star, Bruce Ismay
is standing proud and smiling in the dock.
*Twenty-two knots, yes sir!* he assures us. Nearer New York
to Thee. Blue Riband in his eyes, a smile.
We are still at Crozier, listening to the wind rivet
its Ross Sea Dreadnought, Unsinkable,
to be sent north next spring, parade tiptoe
in front of millionaires and aristocrats who'll have it
photographed and still not picture the unthinkable,
the cold, the dark, the seven eighths below.


30

I'm awake at the crack, but not of dawn. Once I woke
to hear the same noise, in February – ponies at the oats,
I thought. Dark then, too. A thin mist. Then this vague rocking,
and, gradually, the long black tongues poking out of the floes
as far as the eye – and Guts had gone! The rest we had to make
jump, before they'd drifted or slipped off and were swallowed
into those hideous jaw-crevasses. Again now the creak.
It freezes me in soaked sweat, the heaving groans
of the pressure-ridge. You expect at any moment the bilious
motion, the black openings to be licking the split pack,
your gear sunk, your tent stranded, the corvine killers
sidling under you ... Then the cold coughs: it's winter, relax.
Today you only have to manhaul two huge loads
through the pitch dark, across concealed crevasses, towards

31

Another time, when there was a lake here, warm
with fish life, palms round it, emerging species
struggling out, and before that, before the slopes of beech
and conifer, before the snail even, before the worm,
in earliest Jurassic, when the earth's womb
was trailing afterbirth, and the red screech
which was life had wriggled, unloved, unleashing
its wild schemes to expand and overwhelm
its feverish, exhausted mama – imagine …
And in a couple of million centuries' time,
us, sitting in our tent atop that blue shining
mile-deep history of heat and raging
blizzards, chafing dead limbs at a primus,
on the point of succumbing to evolution.


32

We are caricatures who box between the slits
in the spinning rim of a toy. We are spun
to re-enactment on this wheel, for the fun
of experiencing continual defeat. Among the exhibits
in the Crystal Palace, beneath the curving lights
with organ and wind machine, in wax: Birdie,
Cherry, and Bill. The tableau, *Victorian Murderers*
is next to ours, *Edwardian Suicides*.
There is no getting away, there's little hope
of ever getting out of this. It was a hazardous
undertaking. Not heroes, three foolish men.
We are small figures in a crystal globe
turned upside down and shaken to a blizzard
by a child, who laughs, and shakes it again.

## 33

'A stranger I came out here, a stranger I go back.'
The summer months amused us. We watched the sea-ice crack.
The papers spoke of heroes. Our leader of the Pole.
But now we feel these ice-jaws devour our very soul.
It's every day and all day, or else our fuel won't last.
In darkness, minus seventy, we haul against the blast.
The moon and cloud in conference allot a gleam or two.
A glimpse of guttering footholds, black smudges in the blue.
For God's sake why put up with this? It's going to drive us mad.
Those penguin cries will haunt us. Their eggs will all be bad.
My blank thoughts are irregular. My breath has turned to rhyme.
I'll close my verse behind me, and I may be out some time.
Have cut a final ditty for the public as I walked.
A valedictory spiral. To be sung the way I talked.

## 34

Glockenspiel, wind machine, and wordless chorus.
Closer, shuddering the diaphragm, closer time cuts
the groove, records our Sinfonia Heroica.
Glockenspiel, wind machine, and wordless chorus.
Icicles of string begin the lament in A minor.
We are beneath the knife, we can feel this
cancer cut from our throats, we have seen into the abyss.
Icicles of string begin the lament in A minor.
A Christian soul from deep within the ice-fall
summons us. Absurd, our hurdy-gurdy
tune grinds on: *auf dem Eise*
*wankt er hin und her*  Go forth upon thy journey
Christian soul, from deep within the ice-fall,
*und sein kleiner Teller bleibt ihm immer leer*

35

All is well. I shall simply – I have no regret –
I shall simply fall and go to sleep in the snow –
except in leaving you to struggle through alone –
mere faith, mere absolute faith that even that
is all for the best. I'd like to have seen your latest letters.
Dad's little compass and Mother's little comb
are in my pocket. I had wanted to send news home
but we'll all meet after death, death, death is
all is well. We have struggled to the end. What matters
we have done what we thought was best. My own
dear wife, goodbye, God be warm to you, blow
kiss, wind, crack, and a cheer from Cherry: the hut is
straight ahead. Then have I slept twice sixty-seven miles?
Or Heaven is a hut, hot cocoa, familiar smiles.


36

One day in nineteen-ten I had a fleeting vision.
I saw in imagination a solemn pagan rite,
sage elders seated in a circle watching
young men march themselves to death.
One day in nineteen-eleven it was dark
and I heard Corinthians read, and an arrangement
of St Matthew played to a Coronation March,
my friends pictured in tombs within Westminster.
One day after nineteen-twelve has passed,
the pressure to obey one steadfast finger
will have crushed my craving for the solitary wastes
into a pungent relish for adventure
of any sort, so off to a trench in Flanders.
*Es ist nichts als der Winter, es ist nichts als der Winter.*

*Arbroath, 1981*

## BABY-ARCTIC

These young parents
plotted their love
between true poles,
but now there's a baby

magnetic north

and the line of attention
drawn between them
suddenly swings to him

and aurora borealis
shrieks them awake
or a star's breath becalms them
on drugged black somnolence.

The intangible existence
in that white unfocused gaze
is the frozen aim of these months
marching through terrain
undreamt of, wild, implacable.

At each unknown camp they erect
a tent of snug devotion,
open their concentrates,
eat, sing, play,
keep the cold out
and leave a colour photo
waving from the blank like a flag.

Though to colour-blind eyes
progress is lost
against the wind-emptied plains
of the baby-arctic,
the instruments of parental care
lovingly rule
on a lifescale chart
each new line
towards the filial north.

*1979*

# EGYPT

## (1979–)

*for Alan Bolesworth and Stuart Evans*

## WESTERNERS

we ferried our past across here
our furniture    our favourite things
the familiar parts of our life

we reconstructed them to make
ourselves an opulent future
and barricade oblivion

you will recognise us among
these everlasting earth treasures
in a gold mask    or in black granite

in the clean slot of a hieroglyphic
though you thought we were dead and strange
you will recognise us    we are

still here    we are the westerners

## AMENOPHIS IV ADDRESSES THE THEBAN PRIESTHOOD

as we are

not stiff
with authority

or fixed upright
in our thrones

beside decrepit
and obscure symbols

but like this

leaning out of a window
with my wife

to exchange a word or two
with a passer-by


equal
on whom
the Aten
shines


you have known this
for as long
as the gods have been absent
from within your walls

but have concealed it
behind the obeisant
mirage, seductress Maat

truth, she says,
persuading the people
to bend down like ostriches


now look at the
face of the man in the moon

at a cat's eyes
at a nose long and ridiculous

as it meets these protuberant lips
with a snub   and my hips

that are round
like a woman's


and witness

the ideal
you froze

in a thousand
colossal blocks

in a million
blank imaginations

melt here
in the hands of Truth


I am King


but I wear the royal kilt
pleated like a dial
to catch the sun's rays

I stand
in electrum
and shout

on the horizon
of the horizon
of the sun-disc


Akhenaten
Servant of the Sun

and never
shall he step

beyond this boundary
beyond this place of purity

## NEFERTITI IN THE NORTH

Not to be closer
to the roots
of this rose

in lands
where they say the Nile
no longer flows

but falls
like the sunlight

not to be watching
the bird-catchers
crouch
where the gardens end
outside my window

and that same figure
on my wall

not for the paintings
of his nets and his dog
driving from the papyrus thickets
a slim-necked water-fowl

not for these

and not to be quenched
by the sight
of the sand's disregard
for his sacred boundaries

never to scoff in triumph

'the-beautiful-woman-has-come'
has come

but since the King
is in the south
in the company
of his dear Smenkhare

I have come
to this castle in the north


## THE CRACK

The Pharaoh has arrived in Aswan today:
being cheered off the barge, being greeted
by officials from the quarry, on his way

through the streets, luxuriously seated
in a palanquin, to supervise the long-planned
raising up of his newly completed

obelisk. Across desert, up the grand
triumphal causeway carved for this occasion,
he's escorted to where the workmen stand,

their faces smooth, as if the abrasion
of a fear, of a persistent nightmare,
had ground them away. Without expression,

they watch their foreman whisper in an ear
and the quarry official gasp, fall dumb
and helpless and leave the foreman to steer

the guest away. He knows the worst must come,
but he can patch time, pointing out the vast
unyielding rock face and outlining some

of the problems caused by having to work fast
and make crucial cuts too quickly, with risk
of ruin ... Leading the falcon eye past

the hollow of a previous obelisk
which only the rock's good temper had meant
it was finished and erected in weeks ...

But the Pharaoh has begun his ascent:
lifted over the rock these men wrestled
to overthrow, shaded from rays they spent

long months exposed to, some of them pressing
the wooden wedges in the hard-worked slots
and dampening them to swell, some dressing

the hacked-out shape for the final cuts –
and all, even through the pink rock-dust, pale
as alabaster now, aware of what's

made out to quarry employees who fail
to finish their allotted task before
the Pharaoh comes. Today, it's a fairy tale.

But that day it was as if the earth's core
had pumped a deep black vein of evil up
out through the granite slab, and the men saw

the crack, as if they were watching a heart stop.

## 'WELCOME AT ASWAN'

We have seen the sights.
What's left?

the mausoleum in my head
the broken obelisk in our bed
the reconstruction of all I've said
on your separate island

and ahead

the yellow drifts of the dead
the days bereft
and the long rock nights


## SHAM EL-NESSIM
*(the smell of the west wind)*

I

When the wind blows
from the west
it doesn't blow fresh air

but the debris

dust of a noble
and the pigments he chose
to decorate his tomb

choking specks

the decayed ritual
of daily life

II

When the wind blows
across the water

it back-combs
a Nubian widow's hair

and discovers streaks of white
in the black waves


III

When the wind blows
along the new corniche

and sends the white hats
flying off the red faces

and the red dresses
waving
above the white legs
of western girls

it swells
the felucca boy's
lateen eyes

and propels him
from the Hapi
to the Grand Hotel

'Monsieur want boat?
Ah, boat?
Felucc'?'

and on
until at the Cataract

'Boat?
Want sailing boat?'

it grounds him
sweeping his appeal
into the desert

with the body-sweat
coach-exhaust and kitchen
smell of the west wind


## A Date from Nubia

More than whisky warms
the heart on a balmless

February night,
Shukri, creaking to the gate

in a thin gallabeya
and a gone-home pair

of my old socks
warms it with his jokes

and his devilish winks
as he smiles 'ideeni whisky!'

and we slap hands and laugh.
But he wouldn't touch the stuff,

he's a Nubian, the Koran
on his lap. In Ramadan

he won't swallow
his saliva, let alone

a scotch. When he prays,
it's five times down on his knees

at dawn, at noon,
in the afternoon, when the sun's

just gone, and in the evening.
If a stranger should ring

and interrupt him, he'll welcome
you with tea and then resume

from scratch, but only after
insisting you accept the offer

of a date – saying, except
fresh like gold dropped

from the palm you could chew
to the breathing of the buffalo

water-wheels, he has no taste
for them himself; but a guest

like you, who's off
to Abu Simbel or to photograph

the High Dam, must eat
one dried date

as a commemorative act:
the last time dates were picked

in Nubia, Shukri had
teeth, and Nasser wasn't dead.

## HOWARD CARTER AT SWAFFHAM

We know him: it's
the Carter lad who
painted dear Lady
Amherst's lap-dog

and the Vicar's old
bull-terrier, quite
without schooling – son
of our gamekeeper's son.

And if his imagination
pierces a tiny hole
in these venerable walls
and holds a candle

through to a room full
of wonderful things
but utterly foreign to
a decorously mounted

hunting party with
its fine equipage,
its whips and sticks and
stuccoed wooden courtesy –

then what is that to us?
Tally-ho! and on towards
the twentieth century: let
the boy be content

with keeping trespassers
from our noble pile;
or immortalise our
ailing Golden Retrievers.

## CARTER'S DESCENT
*(February 1924)*

To come down these sixteen steps
holding the keys, the sole keys,
and hearing the reverberation from
that heavy iron grille; to know
that not even the *Times* correspondent
can follow me here ...
                  To come down
and enter the darkness and to see
through the darkness a cracked lid
still suspended above that
most public, most secret mask, not
shaped to reflect either the lunacy
of a heretic predecessor or a star-
blind sacerdotage, but to glow
below the horizon of the sun-disc
modestly – no papyri, no press ...

To come down where everyone has appeared
to understand why their hands must be tied,
their heads bowed, their tongues slit –
why everything (chariot, ostrich feather
fan, mere child's toy) must be restrung
along my endless, exact, but unbreakable lines ...

To come down where I have felt
alive and in command as if
it had been my own kingdom and I
liberated from fake courtesies
(permission denied/permission granted),
gilded wooden minds, hollow talkers ...

To come down and handle a reed basket
of three thousand years ago, and forget
the three thousand unanswered letters
in my identical basket –
                  *Surely you must be*
*our long lost cousin from Camberwell ... ?*
*Might this perhaps cast light on the crisis*

*in the Congo ... ? Just send me a gold bar*
*or two – some mummy cloth – some of the beer*
*dregs – a grain of sand – I enclose half*
*a crown ...*
                    To come down
to where the responsibility and the doubt
do not hang on their frayed ropes
like halves of that granite lid
cracked by a priest's men in antiquity,
lifted through the power of the English aristocracy,
abandoned to a rotten Egyptian bureaucracy ...

Carnarvon – you would have smiled,
you would have gone out and shot a few hundred
rabbits or opened a magnum and toasted one
of two kings, or rested on this barbaric couch
before hurrying down to your beloved darkroom ...

Carnarvon – your dog, your favourite dog,
howled and died with all the lights of Cairo
that April morning ...
but the high, clear air of Beacon Hill
was golden, as they buried you, with lark song.

At noon, under the desert sun, I discover
steps that lead deep into myself.

To come down to this dark
and to know that after the long
bolero brays its climax
and the final veil of bullion
has been lifted, there will be sudden
leather and tooth and rag,
and the same bejewelled ignorance
as when we began –
                    is to come down
to earth, is to come down
to brass tacks, is to come down
carrying heavy iron keys
and to leave with a glimpse
of the golden ankh.

## THE TREASURES OF TUTANKHAMUN
*The British Museum, 1972*

I am waiting, like all the others, waiting
to open the sacred seal and discover
my future; and as I wait, this exhibition
snakes me through steel barriers to my golden
eighteenth year where I catch, amid the darkness
that enfolds a teenage Pharaoh's history,

glimmerings of a more personal history,
as if it had lain beneath the sand waiting
for me to come and dig into its darkness
in search of the famous Mask but discover
only in each glass case my own face, golden.
It is my coming-of-age exhibition.

All aspects of me are in this exhibition:
the child's chair and board-game are a history
of my early youth; my teens were that golden
dagger. This trumpet, this cow-bed are waiting
for me to experiment, to discover
in their cross-meshed passages of darkness,

in sexual unity and divine darkness,
the Goddess Hathor's milk-white exhibition
of her transfiguring powers: discover
between her lyriform horns all history.
The Necklace of the Rising Sun is waiting
to embrace us, its clasp is cool and golden …

Each morning my hopes shoot greener, but golden
futures only bloom after months in darkness,
during nights of counting the weeks of waiting,
and now at this jubilee exhibition
I am persuaded that time and history
are relative. Come, UCCA! and discover

to me the sacred light, let us discover
the place where we are to spend our golden
prime and inscribe our names on history
as one young man did, emerging from darkness
at eighteen to become this exhibition –
the very thing for which we are all waiting.


## THE DAY I FOUND KING TUT

Opposite the British Museum
just along from Coptic Street
is Davenports,
the magicians' shop.

I used to get their catalogue
sent and crept nightly
into the treasury:
fans, flowers, Floating

Zombies, Find the Lady,
Funny Bunny, Indian
Rope Trick, Chinese Rings –
and on the back page

all I could afford,
the after-dinner jokes:
a blue plastic coffin
with a red plastic

'King Tut' lying
quite snugly, held
by a concealed magnet,
which, with a sleight

of hand, you could
dislodge so that
like-poles repelled
and the Pharaoh would

not lie down, would
not lie down, only
you the arrogant
thirteen-year-old

knew how! I was
a regular mummy's
curse from the day
I found King Tut.

*1987*

# OMM SETY

*Omm Sety is the name adopted by Dorothy Eady (1904–1981), an English woman who
became convinced, after a bad fall at the age of three, that she was in reality an Ancient
Egyptian priestess from the Temple of Abydos. Eventually, a series of startling encounters
led her to realise that she had been (and was to be again) the mistress of the Nineteenth
Dynasty Pharaoh Sety I. Omm Sety spent the latter years of her life in Abydos, a legendary
figure amongst all those who lived or worked in Egypt. This poem interweaves an oblique
narrative of her life history with 'songs' and commentary from Sety himself: there are also
two somewhat irreverent monologues for the deities Isis and Osiris. I have incorporated
various Egyptian elements into the structure and stanza-form of the poem, using the design
of the Osirion at Abydos and the so-called 'djed'.*

SETY I, OSIRIS, ISIS, HORUS

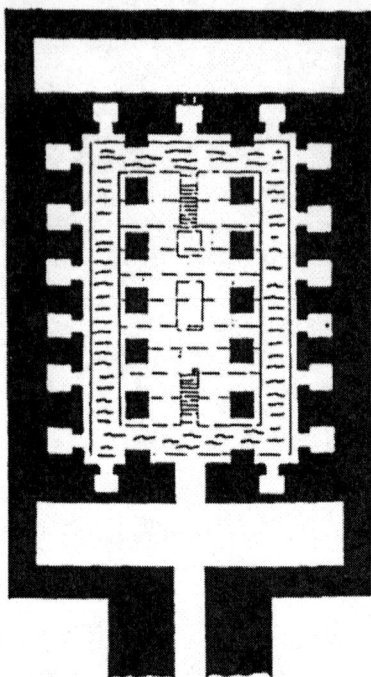

THE OSIRION AT ABYDOS

SETTING UP THE DJED
*From a Bas-Relief at Abydos*

She
is falling down an endless flight.
The beak-nosed doctor
arrives and kneels – a mirror – a feather –
makes a note, then lifts
her back up the stairs (so heavy!)
to her fresh-painted nursery
in Blackheath. *Dorothy, you say?* He notes
the time. *And she was three?*
It is 1907 and death
in infancy is commoner still
than teenage trench fever.
Shell-shocked, her parents
know the correct form,
first draw the curtains,
order the black crape
for Mr Eady (Master
Tailor) to sew up
his own daughter's funeral. Now the doctor
is returning with a nurse and a death certificate.
He holds a quill out formally for the signature
then enters the nursery for the washing of the corpse –
finds it sitting up and covered with chocolate.

*Sweetness. A desert seed long baked*
*beneath the sand begins to break*
*and bud and climb. King Sety stirs*
*and rises as a ninth life purrs*
*into his heart. My heart. For I*
*am Sety, soul that will not lie*
*in peace until it finds that face*
*three thousand spirallings of space*
*have hidden, since in Abydos*
*where priests had gathered to rehearse*
*their virgins in the sacred play*
*of Isis I first saw her – may*
*you gods forgive my sacrilege,*
*but let the Council be my judge.*
*A heart hangs above your fiery well.*
*Sety lost his balance. Sety fell.*

                    She
        is always crying, crying to go home
               – *But you* are! *This* is!
        unable to express where home might be
               if not in Blackheath
        at the black hub of the British Empire
               its slaves hauling huge
        grey statistics across white foolscap
               until she is taken by her parents
               to the British Museum (solely
               because she would be trouble
               if left) – bored, petulant,
               dragging her heels from gallery
               to gallery – not interested
               in the Elgin marbles, nor
               in Babylonian harps, not
               jade, not ivory, nor any
               of the spoils of war, until
        granite clenches a flame, and hurls
        the girl to answer its riddle, to kiss
        its paws, to embrace a long-lost cocoon,
        refusing to budge, but croaking an aged:
        *Leave me! These are my people!*


A good old man, *the people lied,*
*and swiftly buried me in state.*
*My failures safely mummified,*
*they dubbed my young successor 'Great' …*
*They knew I'd suffered, saw I tried*
*to build but fell beneath this weight*
*that pressed and crushed my earthly pride*
*till all I had were Mysteries*
*from Abydos. Well deified*
*with precious goods and precious words*
*I woke – and on the farther side*
*of the false door I thought I heard*
*my Harp-of-Joy … But no. I cried*
*that all I found were starlit roads*
*where time could run or stop or hide*
*from those who plumb her Mysteries.*

She
dreams of a garden glimpsed through the stony
frown of parent and teacher –
till Abydos smiles up at her from a heap
of Illustrated London News:
– *That is my home! That is the garden where I lived!*
– *Lies, Dorothy! There are no*
*gardens in the desert.* In 1914
the ancient approaching this
ten-year-old (who's skipped
her dancing class to come
in secret to the Museum) is hardly
the warrior-hero she desires,
but as unique a museum piece
as the scarab ring on its soft
plump white hand –
content to leave trench
digging to younger men.
Sir Wallis Budge. *Hieroglyphs, eh? Try*
*'Thou shalt exist for millions of years,*
*a period of millions of years'. Do you see?*
She sees, but not the bombing, as he heaps
jewels from a royal cemetery on her head.

*The paths led on for years, beyond*
*the Black through Red and desert lands,*
*to icy planets, shrunken stars,*
*for centuries. With empty hands*
*I came back to the Council,*
*to rumours you were 'sleeping in*
*the blackness', practising rebirth,*
*that when you were awake, my* ka
*might be allowed to visit earth.*
*News came back from the Council.*
*Word had it, I would find you now*
*upon a shore of silvery rain.*
*Yes, I could go – not as I am*
*but wrapped in mummy cloth again,*
*without a heart, without a brain,*
*then come back to the Council.*

She
has survived the bombing of her dancing class
and come to Plymouth, where
the century will unreel its horrors behind her:
Kaiser Wilhelm's strut,
Kitchener's finger, the King's eyes.
She steps up before the screen
of her father's pride, the New Palladium,
and hums away her childhood
to the one tune that haunts her –
*The Lament of Isis and Nephthys*
shaken into the dark
and smoke of peacetime, seeing
only a dazzling sun,
feeling only the organ's
moody throb, while the heat
is melting her father's philanthropic
blocks of ice, her eyes
blurring the three thousand … CUT!
as a gigantic mask projects itself
upon the black. Sety. The dead stare
of a mummy. Sety the First. And a white
nightdress torn from neck to hem.

*The Council will pass judgment soon*
*on who disturbed the finely tuned*
*balance between gods and man.*
*They ruled the King might walk. He ran.*
*They ruled the King might look. He touched.*
*Magnanimous, they granted much,*
*but I took more. Let Sety pay*
*this heavy price, that while they weigh*
*my heart, yours is released again*
*to rock the scales of living men.*
*The Law says life's course must be run.*
*The sun is set. Long live the son.*
*My one hope now is in your eyes.*
*They give me faith he might yet rise*
*who sinks to think you have not heard*
*one syllable of this last word.*

She
reads what the Egyptians have to say about our empire's
rape of her sacred valleys.
She gathers her entire collection of artefacts
bought with dancing money
and dispatches all to Cairo with a note:
'Render unto Caesar …'
then skips upstairs to wash her hands
and in the basin seeing
the four-sided well
in the tree-lined garden
and her dripping hands become
a winged shadow, she
knows the water from this
imperial plumbing is poison
compared with that pure
source in the desert of her dream
that is still clearer now
the guilt has lifted. As she undresses
she wonders: will he come? Or was it
imagination? Abuse? Beyond the glass
hawk and fox, the standing stones
of the moor. Tomorrow she will return.


She
is in London again, looking for the dream
in a House of Commons debate
where everyone is sleeping, sleep-talking –
*Does the Honourable Member*
*agree that Egypt must at all costs*
*remain a vital organ*
*of the British Empire?* Much nostril
projection as her mind
and the mind of one Imam
beside her on the bench
unite in the other world
of democratic process
and shadow names like Hitler,
Mussolini, Stalin

ripple the bland snore
of nineteen thirty-three.
She agrees to marry him
and settle, not in Abydos, not even
close to the Nile or any monuments
but among colonials, a fashionable shrine
in which to have a child called Sety
and wait each night for his namesake to return.

*With the breath of*
*the north wind*
*I have come to you –*

*with Dorothy, O Wizard*
*of Everlastingness:*
*Ozymandias's father's girl,*

*a whirlwind to stir*
*the dust from*
*your name. Have some*

*forgotten you? O Lord*
*of All the Gods whom the Lords*
*of All the Lands once praised –*

*yes, most will have*
*some difficulty putting*
*a name to your face.*

*But the god of writing*
*is bringing you to light,*
*has reconstructed you, through*

*the sands of his wisdom,*
*the dust of his observation,*
*the dryness of his wit –*

*Thoth, in other words,*
*has talked a poet into*
*commemorating you.*

*But you would prefer to crawl*
*into a chest, say yes*
*to whatever mad*

*relatives want, and wake up*
*dead while the tanks*
*roll on above. You went*

*to pieces. Wanted to bury*
*your head and hope it would all*
*blow over. Admit it. Well,*

*there's peace now. So let*
*this fresh air puff*
*the seed of your greatness*

*into the garden at Abydos.*
*Assist the girl. I remain*
*your humble shadow.*

### I

*divorce you* is all a man has to say,
three times, and Sesame!
It wasn't my affair with the Antiquities Department
(common knowledge) and not
that I could never explain to my parents-in-law
who the man was they saw
at night on my bed – how when he comes
a thick pane of glass
lies between us, when he speaks
the glass is a Rosetta Stone
of triple meanings, lost
connections. The air-raids
that bomb-cratered my puberty
have gone, thank the gods. Only
my warrior-hero calls
to his Harp-of-Joy to play
in the garden of figs and vines –
No, the sin was that I could not cook.
My kushari was like an unguent you might use
to preserve a king, but not a husband.
He liked the modern. I the ancient.
He took young Sety. I keep the old.


### I

awoke to find I was not in bed
but lured out by Sety
to the Great Pyramid. *Follow*, he said
and started to climb the eastern
face until halfway he stopped and loosened
a stone as if to say –
That's all. Go home. Sleep. When I
awoke my feet were dusty
and as I passed the pyramid
that morning there where a
block was moved in my head
burnt a blue light
for all to see and say
this has been witnessed before,

misfortune's harbinger,
since history began. That night,
my head on my pillow, I
awoke to the cry of women and the news came:
a man had fallen from the Great Pyramid,
a worker, sweeping the sand from the steps
on the eastern side, when halfway up
he stumbled. I lay back and slept.

*Whoever climbs and finds the foothold gone –*
*unbalanced, tumbling through a night*
*of jackals, vipers, scorpions and cats –*
*such are the feelings of the lover left alone.*
*Harp-of-joy, I play you as the wind*
*plays on tightened nerves, like the hamseen*
*that flings its yellow dust-sheet over spring*
*and makes the ardent harpist's music blind.*
*Whoever turns keen eyes towards a star*
*and finds the clouds obscure their view*
*but makes of cumuli a lovelier show,*
*they know just what my feelings are –*
*Harp-of-joy, I play you as the years*
*play Theban stone, as the Colossus*
*of Memnon or Amenophis, that once used*
*to sing at sunrise, has no voice, but hears.*

I

longed to spend the night in that tomb
where some of the mummies were.
I pleaded with my ex to use his influence
(that modern magic word)
and he succeeded, so long as I was in
by eight and not out
until sunrise. Fine. I came with a vacuum
and joined the velvet covered
cases for the night. Lifting
each veil in turn,
I found at last the shell
of my first love. No eyes
but a haughty brow, and lips
about to kiss, a chin
determined to outlive Orion
still wheeling across
unseen, indifferent to both
live loving flesh or parchment.
But always the glass between us. I lay down –
on one side, Sety; Ramesses the other –
and dreamt of my pets, my vipers, that falcon
that follows me even to this abandoned tomb.

*You knelt and smiled at my last smile,*
*my glory's slough, my power's shell,*
*as if you still could not believe*
*the body's merely where we live.*
*Yet I have taken you in dream*
*beyond the painted walls of time*
*to show you scepticism's cure.*
*The Council is well pleased with your*
*achievements, and they now confirm*
*Ptah Mes, a minor priest, may come*
*to fetch you. Here, we will design*
*a future for our past, and train*
*this love whose roots tap down into*
*the Middle Kingdom, how to fruit*
*when our short flowering season ends.*
*What nature separates, love binds.*

I
am a curiosity, respected for my ideas, but laughed at
for my origins – I don't mean
that original vegetable seller's daughter
the King squeezed to see
if she was ripe – but my father, the tailor
turned cinema proprietor,
climbing out of his cloth bindings into the light.
I was brought up a priestess
of the dark temple, dressed
as became a virgin, learning
to sing, to dance, to act
a role in *The Mystery of Isis,*
*The Resurrection of Osiris,*
so popular each season
at Abydos, the crowds flocked
to Sety's temple, the Nineteenth
Dynasty's New Palladium.
At three, I had stumbled and fallen down into
the discovery that everything was of paint and canvas,
strutted and braced, even the light artificial,
the lines typed. Some girls' dream is of
a ticket to Hollywood. Abydos, mine.


I
suppose I should explain before time runs out
why it took me until
the Year of Revolution to get around to Abydos.
In one sense I was already there.
It began with a visitation from a young priest,
escorting me out of my body
to an L-shaped room (the L for Learner, perhaps)
where Sety repeated the story
of his three millennia quest
to find a girl he knew
for an hour in the temple garden,
who killed herself out of guilt
and fear. His fruitless efforts
at visiting in mummy form,

and those other dream encounters
before Imam divorced me.
    Now, he said, he was at liberty
to come at last in his most solid form,
and youthful, to middle-aged me, if I
would only give my consent and (the rub!) a pinch
of my essential spirit. A small price
for that night's taste of his prowess.

*Peace, you say,*
*but I'm still waiting*
*for the one essential piece*

*you claim you haven't*
*been able to track down.*
*I don't know if I trust you.*

*Oh, we can manage?*
*You've been saying that*
*for how many millennia?*

*And all we've produced*
*thus far is a fluttering*
*falcon. If I had known*

*appeasing my brother*
*would set the pattern*
*not for peace*

*but for the dissection of*
*all I hold dear – Kalabsha,*
*Philae, Abu Simbel –*

*because some neo-Cheops*
*has said Dam*
*the Inundation …*

*Why will they still try*
*to impress us with their*
*huge erections?*

*You wish me to respond*
*to this child in the garden*
*at Abydos, to allow*

*fool Sety to have*
*his perverse desire,*
*and yet I am deprived*

*of my own penis*
*because you cannot be*
*bothered to look*

*any further! Oh, a fish*
*has eaten it now?*
*I wish it joy of it.*

*Why should I get up*
*for you anyway?*
*I see no signs of peace.*

We
omitted to see Omm Sety during our stay
and only by staring hard
now at a photo of the Osirion do those seventeen
chapels, ten pillars
and two drowned subterranean shrines
begin to re-emerge. We came
the year of the peace floodgates. She
the year the canal was claimed,
hoping to locate her garden
and her one god, but expelled
by Eden and his war angels,
more friendly with the cobras
that inhabited the temple than
with her compatriots, determined
to prove the existence of that
paradise by finding the walls
of a man-made channel
or by walking in the pitch-black to whatever point
the Chief Inspector of Antiquities might pick,
playing their game to prove she had lived
on this site, had knowledge that there would be fruit
and vine roots, the remains of a canal, proof.


We
*had a flu epidemic,* she explains. *I felt*
*dizzy as I left the temple*
*and fell against the wall to a loud*
*grating sound, and found*
*I was rolling away into darkness. Light*
*began to gossamer down*
*and I saw the beak of Horus as he bent …*
Another of her tumbles into
the surreal. Dust clears
and the rational takes shape.
Of course it wasn't Horus
but his statue. She had stumbled on
a hoard beneath the Hall
of the Sacred Boats, and although

it is never to be seen again,
guards notice cobwebs
on Omm Sety's hands –
Gone, like her dream, like her childhood, like that horse,
her only friend, Mut-ho-tep, as a girl.
Gone. Her golden steed is an ass
that treads the ridge between two worlds
in parallel. At any moment she might fall.

*And I will catch you once again.*
*Why linger in this haunt of men?*
*Your path leads to Amenti, here*
*where truth is featherlight and clear*
*and meaning is not mummy-bound*
*but made of love, the purest sound*
*a blind immortal harpist plays*
*from depths beyond unseeing eyes*
*where dancers dressed in midnight sun*
*spin into the stars, till none*
*can tell which are the nebulae*
*and which the patterns of their play*
*and everlasting life is full*
*with starlight wine, with magical*
*inebriations of the tongue,*
*my Harp-of-Joy, my solar-strung.*

We
would like to thank Omm Sety for her guidance,
for her wise advice that we
women who want children should first make an offering
to Hathor at the ninth pillar,
that we men who want children should bury
a pyramid text written
on a goose egg at our thresholds, and we
who have seen cobras tamed
with a whispered *Seb-EN!*
and scorpions driven out
by the placing of a small stone,
who have seen her pray
to Osiris for revenge and watched
retribution follow – a death
from rabies or heart attack –
but witnessed also a child
cured by a cup of water
from the well in the Osirion that she saw gurgling
in a shaft of white light, the same well
whose droplets she used to clear her own long-
sightedness, she who chose to live with no
running water, in a reed hut, alone.

*But not – assure them – not alone.*
*Explain that to their sacred* ankh,
*their wedjet – 'lens' or 'microphone'.*
*So much we shared is silent, blank.*
*But you were not alone, for he,*
*your soul-mate Sety, made provision,*
*knew your needs. We hold the key*
*of life. Tell that on 'television'.*
*Unblind all those whose hours are paved*
*with traps of untouchable distraction*
*to how their riches have deceived.*
*They watch their own* ka *burn in action.*
*Only those whose hours are years,*
*whose years are centuries of love*
*behold what patient nurture rears.*
*From seed below. The flower above.*

*We*
*have heard so much about you, Omm Sety*
*and seen you on TV ...*
– A relief from all that pornographic stuff.
I will show you the temple.
Prithee, come. Observe here how the phallus
has been blotted out, because
so many have taken fragments for their potency –
Now you can see the jackal
Wepwawat bestowing
crook and flail on Sety.
These are guides to show
the newly dead the route
from here to the Kingdom of Osiris.
Where is that? Beyond
the West. A jackal's prints
will lead you out of the desert
to fertile land. Look –
how the light here gives this relief a green
translucence. Do you sense the benevolence, serenity
sprouting from these papyrus columns? *Is it true –*
*Sety – that he – that even now he ... ?* Children,
do not believe all that you see in the box.

*Do not deny me to your people.*
*Must I send the stones*
*tumbling from these walls*
*to crush such chips of arrogance?*
*Do not deny me to your people.*
*Must I open these lids*
*and sear with primal beams*
*such motes so lazily guided?*
*Do not deny me to your people.*
*Must I unwind the West*
*until the touch of death*
*reprograms all that once amused?*
*Do not deny me to your pupils.*
*Trust your own eyes to see*
*our temple, our garden, our well.*
*Believe in the sense of Sety.*

We
were packing all our souvenirs and gifts
for the flight back home
when you set out on your voyage to Amenti,
Omm Sety. We had stayed
two years, our poorest and our richest,
you – half a century
of intercourse across thirty centuries.
Scent or strain of music,
gesture, profile, touch,
that last glance back –
like paintings in the Tomb of
the Remainder of our Lives, just one
false door, marked
POETRY, to allow the *ka*
to come and go as now
it does, remembering that day
in 'eighty-one, when –
did we even hear about it? We were too busy
arranging who would take our cat, a note
in our diary says she was very nervous, it was
'an odd evening'. We said goodbye to our friends
resting our eyes again on the West Bank.

*Leave your cats, your Teti-Sheri,*
*your Hor-em-heb: on this last ferry*
*no Ramesses, Ankhsi, Ahmes, Mery.*
*Your animals will sing to you.*
*Leave your gander, leave your goose,*
*Snofru, Nebet, set them loose.*
*You need no watch on your new house.*
*Your animals will sing to you.*
*Leave your rabbit, leave your dog*
*Khalouli. Surely leave that frog*
*called Pharaoh to his monologue.*
*Your animals will sing to you.*
*Leave your birds, your peregrine.*
*Like these vipers, shed your skin.*
*My horse Mut-ho-tep calls you in.*
*Your animals all sing to you.*

We
who love her, find a mysterious life
in Abydos: other ears
than mine have heard the music in the halls,
the sistrum, tambourine and pipe.
And other eyes have seen the golden glow
in the Sanctuary of Osiris
when no lamp was lit. And I have stood
alone in Pega-the-gap
at the Great Feast of Osiris
listening to the jackals howl
but at midnight, immediately
the jackals were hushed, a deep
silence fell and I
felt myself surrounded
by a great multitude of people,
heard their breath, their feet
on the sand, and as I passed
through the gates of the Temple of Osiris,
their presence, their breathing, their whispering feet
vanished into the past, and I was left
with only the stars and the cold of ruined
walls, their clear impenetrable text.

*1996*

## THE AMARNA STELAE

At Karnak, who was it unearthed
in nineteen twenty-five
those twenty-five colossi
of Akhenaten? In the photograph
they rise up out of the sand
like science-fiction clones
or giant ivory chessmen
dropped at the end of a game
on a beach in the Hebrides.

They are caricatures of what
these twenty-five years
have made of one who stood
arms folded and holding
a flail to palely control
a class of Egyptian girls.
*After me. What's your name?*
Mr John, Mr John,
where you get pot belly?

Too much of Egypt has gone
to try and reconstruct
determinatives. Look at this
album with half its photos
fallen out, odd inscriptions
above blurred faces; at our
spoilheap of slides and this
ciné we cannot translate
into any blank cartouche.

Voices that cheered the First
Cataract with us or sang us
to Kitchener's Island have fallen
dumb, have dried at their source
to the fixed mummy-smiles
of Tjuyu and Yuya, a mother
and father, her hair plaited,
his mouth opening. My parents
have stopped singing, too.

At the Colossi on the West Bank
where we leaned our hired bikes
and Dad's *ka* went out
of control for lack of sugar
(sugar stirring all about us),
lumps of crumbling figure
guard a temple that has gone,
though a spirit free-wheeled there,
Akhenaten's gold begetter.

Was it love or self that drove us
to escape high priests and viziers,
to find a freer style for our
marriage in that bow of the Nile,
an aim fletched with the Truth
Feather, to penetrate the Window
of Appearance? Glass shimmering
between us. The Priests of Money
putting paid to the experiment.

The Hidden One proclaims
Akhenaten's move was politic,
the sun he worshipped was himself,
his Venusian features, woman's
pelvis, spindly limbs,
curved spine, bent
knees were caused by a disease
which made him blind and led
to such touching scenes of intimacy

with Nefertiti, who was never
exiled to that 'castle in the north'
but changed her name, her sex,
became co-regent, left
posterity and Hitler the face
she wished to show, turning
a blind eye as the wall
came down, and mocking
all other women.

Checkmate. The king is dead.
These stelae mark his boundaries.
We live on as minimalists
dreaming a Tutankhamun
might clear our title to a castle
or fix the roof. Our daughters
breathe the western wind –
but one has asked for a scarab
and one is a worshipper of the sun.

*2004*

# PORTRAITS
## (1980–1987)

*How safe, methinks, and strong, behind*
*These trees have I incamp'd my Mind*

Marvell

## Sy Mui
(from *Boat People*)

Sy Mui is embroidering

her eyes' point enters a wooden o
her breath swells a small stretch of cotton
to a silken bird of paradise
a silken tree of heaven
silk wings on a green silk moth

Sy Mui is embroidering

the shapes blow from her home
ripple her smile
make her fingers gently quiver

the silkworm weaves
with a slow and circular exactness
and the green moth comes to leaf

## Sweet Chestnut

Maturity is to know the star-shakes
in your heart. It is to have turned aside

and, despite the upright and the smooth, gone on
turning. It is to be twisting free of

one's roots, ascending to its very lip
the twin helix. To have observed each year

some fresh disfiguring lump. To have felt
the next ring splitting under the renewed weight

of spring. It is to have seen the spears
lifted, then a spiked mace.

On slopes of ash to have faced the eruption
of your griefs. To have flowered. To propagate.

## WALNUTS

She would plant two saplings.

There would be silence from the burial place,
but in the future, each Christmas,
home-grown walnuts.

                As if a word
picked green had then gone sour,
she flinched – these family crackings
the exposed ends of a nerve-tree.

A figure deep in the pickling jar.
Two daughters coolly hooking brain from skull.
A father and a mother trying to split
their wrinkled shells.

                    There would be silence.
There would be years of fruitlessness.

She would plant two walnuts.

# THE ASH
*in memory of Jack Redon*

the Ash is for you

because of its charcoal buds
because it conceals white magic
because it can hold all winter
creation's keys

because it is tough

because as a spear, a hoop,
a chess-set, a picture-frame,
or a stage brace
it will keep its elasticity

because it can make its own face up

first appearing with ruddy mountain cheeks
then in pale chorus
weeping through Twickenham gardens

then the scarred and grizzled hero
of some grey Norse epic

collapsing
to a sudden curtain

because it is like a chameleon
an old Polonius

because it can smile
heal advertise
mesmerise
and tell tall stories

because it was once Ygdrasil
because it is
the last of the species in our endgame
Jack, the Ash is for you

## THE OAK

Approaching the perimeter, the boy
who dreams of *Down the Bright Stream*, and the man
who knows *Guernica*. The boy who will ask
what oak apples are, and the man who won't
explain that they are tumours. The boy who hopes
to spot a red squirrel. The man who says
they will all prove grey.
                    My childhood and I
may never have danced Hey Derry Down as
our forefathers danced around the oak, but
we have learnt to read the signs that tell us
THESE WOODS ARE PRIVATE.
                        Thick arteries
have thickened until they shiver behind
this ragged blanket. Young companies
of hazel that wriggle their golden tassels
in a lithe floorshow fascinate and stir
the man. The boy looks up at a jigsaw sky.

A Wicked Witch, The Thunderer, or a Phantom?
The words on the wire repeat their one sound.
These woods, These woods – like a stock dove begging –
These woods have danced a navy on their knees,
are War Office Property and have been
since the Ice Age, since the first battering rams.
Five hundred varieties of riddle
and song: the woodpecker attack, plain cuckoo,
or a brace of Cruise. These woods are private,
and since we can read, we shall not trespass.

But words have not yet heard of literacy.
Outlaws, half wild, they will flee with Rimbaud
to the forest, hide there, seem to have helped
manoeuvre your woolly thoughts into a pen –
but then leap out at you, tear at your heart.
They'll not come to your knife, but screech and squeal
like sawmills to be fed.

Robin Hood's Larder.
The Royal Oak. The Parliament Oak.
The Oak of William the Conqueror, and
Harry's Oak. Oaks that were pulpits.
Oaks that were gibbets. Oaks that are jokes and
resemble naked men. The oak that Hitler
gave to a public school. The haunted oaks.
The stranded oaks. The oak of the artist
or poet. The commemorative oaks.
And oaks strapped round for forty feet of circumference
that simply sprang up wild from a roadside hedge.
The oak that was an acorn on an oak
that grew as Christ grew.
                    These words are public
and this side of the perimeter fence.
There have been songs to which no creature knows
the words and words which nothing – not the raven
on Odin's shoulder, not the writing desk
veneered like the chart of a distant sound –
can solve.
            Pieces indistinguishably blue.


Gathered where they dropped but cannot germinate,
brought to the open, free of history,
free of the long shadow, they may be saved
from extinction, which is in every cup.

## THE LISTS OF COVENTRY

Then, it was just a means of arbitration,
ordeal by mass entertainment: two knights,
like glittering exhibition cases, armed,

escutcheoned, and embroidered, their chased
lances quivering at the opposite ends
of a concourse, waiting for the first trumpet

to send painted Swan and Antelope charging
down on painted Mulberry Tree and Lion;
or a more urgent trumpet – like the voice

of a ten-year-old trying to make himself
heard above his advisers, above the mob
writhing around Wat Tyler's corpse – to cry out

'Let me be your leader!', and in a
kingfisher flash of crimson and green-blue
velvet, prevent the bloodshed. A lover

of spectacle and the colourful arts
of peace, King Richard stands up to flourish
words in illuminated filigree

from a goat-hide scroll … and we recollect
that Pathé shot of Chamberlain after Munich;
or a dark-suited, bespectacled John Nott

stumbling through the lists of British losses.

# PORTRAIT OF HENRY V BY AN UNKNOWN ARTIST

Behind the bodkin nose
and shadowy curve

of occiput
is a draw-weight

of thirteen years,
of which the pursed lips

and brass basilisk
eye are sole evidence:

an eye which, seeing
the French emissary

beg consideration
for twelve thousand

women and children
refugees –

stays blind –
though open, as if

it were looking back-
wards and could sense

the grip of a fist
around the neck's

smug folds, or
a paternal tweak

to that monkish crop –
as if it had long known

the source of its pain,
but longed to glimpse,

further back, the figure
without a crown

drawing his
vengeful bowstring.


## FOR THE SIX WIVES

My brother's wife, but only I loved Catherine:
no woman did I ever trouble more
to be the mother of my kingdom's heir,
to consummate my first, my last, desire.
She failed, and still I travel to her, farther
than dreams can ride, into her castle blackness.

While black-eyed, six-fingered Anne, all blackness –
but yellow for the funeral – round Catherine
danced, and so miscarried, leaving me father
to no son, but to the death of More and more.
The French blade of a sonneteer's desire
took off the goggle-eyed brunette, which done, ere

I had half composed a twisting hybrid air
and walked the paths of polyphonic blackness,
I found in fresh green leaves my heart's desire.
Since neither the Marquess Anna, nor Catherine
of Aragon would give, let plain Jane Seymour
be the mother, and I at last the father

to the name of his father's mother's father,
King Edward. Fog clears, sun explodes the air.
Queen Jane lies back exposed on Childbed Moor
bleeding into her last puerperal blackness.
And I must seek a wife, another Catherine,
an Anne. But all I find when I desire

are dreams that buck, a face that cleaves desire,
a Flanders nightmare come to lure me farther
from my senses. Until a fifth, a Catherine
comes pumping down my dropsied, ulcered skin, air
off Venus' mount, bubbling eruptive blackness:
I rise! I sing! – for a breve. For hundreds more

lie in Mistress Catherine's score. And the maw
of Traitor's gate gapes wide. Some say desire
for heads is for maidenheads, that the blackness
gathered in these my good looks proves them father
to impotence, one nine-year-old their heir.
But winch me here, and I will show them, Catherine …

(And you, Catherine, that if you had given more –
bequeathed me one male heir – this one desire
had flamed no farther, the rest been sweet blackness.)

## WHITE CLIFFS

Whistling round into Shakespeare Cliff, where poor
Mad Tom led his blind father to the verge
of devotion, my only daughter saw
from the carriage window the darkness surge
in upon her. I comfort her with talk
appropriate to her three months of light,
sweet nothings such as Lear perhaps once spoke
to his beloved fool, before the night
tunnelled his wits. Still she will not settle.
I would have tried to lull her with that long
blank verse speech of Edgar's if I thought beetle,
chough or crow talked peace. But she wants a song,
so *There'll be bluebirds over...* Searchlights sweep
above these black white cliffs, and she's asleep.

## King Charles on the Solent

*During the last months before his execution,*
*Charles I was a prisoner at Hurst Castle, where*
*he was permitted to walk every day beside the Solent*

Holdfasts of the wrack that the spring tides cast
up to rot in the mud stink like some vast
dead creature. But I am remembering
another shore, and a child stammering
on a kingdom's edge, under his soaked shoe –
pebbles! More pebbles than all the words he knew
by heart from *Metamorphoses*. More pebbles
than even the genealogical tables
he could recite until he slept, and which must
end, he knew, somewhere in sleep. Pebbles washed
by the sea, by those repeated questions
from the horizon. *Before your accession,*
they said, *you must learn to speak.* As if speech
were something one could pick up from the beach.
The first pebble they put into my mouth
was for that 'king', which I couldn't say without
a stutter as of cleaving a stubborn oak.
They jammed it on to my tongue, told me – *Suck!*
I thought it looked like sugar, but it tasted
cold and would never be swallowed. At best it
was a comfort, and I sucked like a man
alone in the desert. So it began …
But there are few pebbles on the Solent,
nor could I find any of sufficient
size or chill or bitterness to cure these
last few words that give me difficulties.
Therefore I choose not to stoop to your will
(I who learned 'king') Master C-C-Cromwell.

## CROMWELL TO HIS WIFE ELIZABETH

Here in God's water-meadow
where the sun dips
like a fox's tail
and rises
dripping rich light
to paint the willows, fens,
and meandering River Ouse,
are there not greens enough?

Here with our children,
here with my darling mother,
and your most devoted maid,
here with these good workers,
good stout oxen,
are there not smiles enough,
Elizabeth,

that you pollute
a room of plain white
with oils
of the world's monarchy?

What is it in these proud faces
that has so fascinated you
that you can sacrifice your good sense
to one crown after another?

Is it because you are not a bit proud
and not at all majestic,
that you feel you have to let
vain shadows of Elizabeth
dance and play
above our scrubbed bed-head?

Or have you heard the Fen
whispering
that I should tear down
one particular face
and replace
his picture with my own –

to hang between your Richard
and your Bolingbroke?
Perhaps it is that you would
like to become Elizabeth
the Second, Elizabeth?

Look at the common people.
Keep your ears muffed and watch them
as they survive in unalleviated flatness.

Now look in your own dear glass,
Elizabeth,
and not at these weak-chinned,
weak-eyed strong men.

## FOR JANE

As love is a word that can look plain foolish
put into verse, it's one I have avoided.
But in our thirteen years must be embedded
some words sentimentality can't polish.

How did we start? Where all affection starts:
in Mumbles, romantic cliff walks, pale sea,
strains of Sibelius, our eyes meet, agree,
and move to the satisfaction of 'hearts' …

No, it wasn't like that – puns and rhymes
lead the student returning home astray,
a tempting short-cut across Swansea bay,
heedless of quicksands, of high-water times.

But at a bus-stop: me plus fiddle-case,
you out of Zanzibar. You off to your Hall,
me back to digs. We shared lectures. That's all
that's true. A tedious coast-road. Your face.

Now zoom slowly towards a lovingly made
egg custard and lines of Milton's paradise
from either side of a substantial slice
of apple crumble; then as the candles fade,

enter the cactus house in Singleton Park
and taste the orchids, let the exotic palms
sweat: do not yet hold hands, but brushing arms,
be sure to walk together home in the dark.

## CHILD

The white, unsplit
finish of her fine
blonde hair is like

those darts of light from
Aldebaran, the bull's
eye, a ricochet

that sings of years
ago when she was
two, perhaps, or one

and could barely speak,
who now knows words
for all things under the sun.

## MIDDLE C

Those piano keys are keys to the doors
you never opened. When in my innocence
I bought you Mussorgsky's *Pictures*, and force-
marched you through The Great Gate, you had the sense
to prefer a Promenade … but, of course,
that's you, to walk the self-effacing way.
Remember Middle C? The girl who looks
down for a keyhole to help her, then one day
she's climbing up to 'perform' (your wry laugh!)
and finds that grand pianos don't have locks.
A moral, yes – but Mum, not even with half
a smile quote me that church bill (*THE MIDDLE ROAD –
THE ROAD TO FAILURE*) and say, 'My epitaph'.
You only followed the way the music flowed.

## TO MAIDEN CASTLE

When your father, to avoid another scene,
took up his black box, left, and climbed alone
to Maiden Castle, all he was hoping for
was peace. It was the late thirties, a Spitfire
being test-flown overhead, along the lane
the telegraph wires making siren sounds.
He wanted to see for himself, he said,
what the archaeologists were up to.
But you knew what he meant. The primal law
of human nature: that relationships
deteriorate, some in fury, some
to a cold war. What is it begins the end?
A mean squabble over a missing brooch,
a dropped ornament? Or your father's books,
those books your mother detested so much
that when he died (*dust-gatherers!* she said)

she threw them out … Was it the books that day?
All those black words.

It wasn't history
that drew him to the Iron Age hill fort,
but musk of an exeat; the licence
to imagine, responsibility
shelved, to look, to photograph, and instead
of sitting long hours at his work scouring
dry lines of a dull proof, to feel the ramparts
break like a Pacific comber against him,
and capture in a light-sensitive frame
the moment.

He would have seen the trenches.
How the brigades floundered. Sir Mortimer
smiling at his skeletons, their scooped out
Neolithic skulls. He must have known too
the barrages. The arsenals. Fragments
of a Venus. Offerings to the bull god
in a thatched temple of Wisdom. Known them,
but never spoken of them. History
was cinema flak.

It was the moment's beams
that he felt sway across and canopy
his threatened mind, its quiet interiors,
its private spaces, clearing them of all
but present sensation.

And only this –
the photograph that he took – still survives
to help you piece his life back together,
as one might, from a brooch or an ornament,
imagine the faintest outline of a race
long vanished, their homes, their preoccupations,
though never the words, the words that spark as
the ornament falls, the brooch goes missing,
or a book is tossed resentfully aside.

# THE COASTAL PATH
## (1987–1989)

*Behold, the sea itself ...*
                                    Whitman

## SEVEN SEA INTERLUDES

I

Childhood is soft chalk: it allows the sea
to erode, almost to break through; were we
forever children, there would be no Midlands,
only sea air, a mirror-line of headlands.


II

Adolescence arrived like a storm beach
overnight, with bodies, much sea-wrack, and each
shingled face turning guiltily from salt
ejaculations to identify a fault.


III

Student days hang like a pantomime horseshoe:
that bay on whose shores we held our barbecue-
debate-cum-dance, loving the tides' motion;
aware, of course, from lectures, of the pollution.


IV

As young couples we kiss to the cliff's edge,
lie down with razorbills on a narrow ledge,
laugh at the lifeguard, laugh at the fishing folk
in their corky craft, the sea is a huge joke.


V

Executive schedules seldom cover
the seaside; only if there's a lover
or a business conference. One buys a yacht.
One moors it in Poole Harbour. The strakes rot.

VI

Parenthood is a final glimpse of the gold
you found on the beach as a one-year-old.
Return to the Landslip: the past gives way
and you are your children, have feet of clay.


VII

A Saga Holiday, perhaps. Promenades
before supper, an evening playing cards.
Images in a land-locked single room
of crossing the bar, stacks, arches; the blown spume.

## THE COASTAL PATH
*a Dorset sketchbook for Gill and Ian*

This morning we were up and out before
it had even dawned on the hotels

that here was a fine day:
by nine, we had carried Katie

down to Lulworth Cove, where a seam
in the membrane protecting

the county of Dorset opens into
a soft clay womb, and the buoys

bob like coloured Easter eggs until
one turns, as you watch, into a frogman.

* * *

Portland Bill is lying ahead of us.
It looks as limp as last night's

party balloon; although the lighthouse
(where Marie Stopes once lived) points

a sharp moral. Impossible to imagine
that drooping vague peninsula

as the potent source of Sir Christopher
Wren's brainchild, of London's

rebirth from the medieval ash,
or of any United Nations building.

* * *

Once a young maiden was forced to go
down to the fossil forest. It was all

giant cycads and maiden-eating
crocodiles. So she escaped, climbed

Bindon to look down in perfect
tranquillity on this lucky horseshoe.

Unluckily, she slipped: and had her
thick skirt not caught – there, where

that red flag is fluttering, tiny as
a Lulworth skipper … (Katie looks up).

\* \* \*

Over the green ridge with a peek-a-
boo and dribbly gums, comes

Durdle Door, that esteemed formation
which features in every school Geography book

and looks like a half-eaten rusk.
Katie has been studiously examining

not it, but prints left by this drizzle
of pilgrims from the Field Study Centre.

She might appreciate their jargoning, too.
The sea pukes: erosive evolutionary processes.

\* \* \*

Some enterprising landowner established
a caravan pound just above this bay:

wandering through it, you are
die-cast into a fifties souvenir.

It's the sort of place young pony tails
swing away to, saying, *I'm not quite sure*

*if we have your size* – row upon row
of green shoe-boxes; and trees that look like

trees printed on the sides of shoe-boxes;
and couples as stout as eastern bloc boots.

* * *

Still chipping away at that final sonnet,
here Keats stepped ashore for the last time:

*I shall be* – (those eternal whisperings)
*I shall be among the English poets* –

or even discover an ichthyosaurus
fossil in the rock, as did a ten-year-old

Lyme Regis girl who told an autograph-
hunting king, *I am well known throughout Europe.*

Names, like sonnets, and scientific
advances, are not so easily made.

* * *

The English language is a spit
of pebbles, shifting gradually

from Chiswell to Chissel to Chesil;
or in nineteenth-century literary floods,

tons of vocabulary deposited all
of a sudden (as in Moonfleet) until

at one end lie the Hardy novels,
and at the other some slight lyrics by Barnes.

'Many a wreck has foundered on this beach,'
says my guidebook (on which I lean).

* * *

George III can be seen on the A353
near Weymouth, not – naturally –

like the Cerne Abbas Giant, his
virility exposed, but in a cocked hat,

on a horse, as if desperate to escape
the Peeping Toms round his bathing machine.

Wisely too, for if he had wanted
to wash his hands on that fashionable prom

today, he would find I AM ACROSS THE ROAD
IN FULL UNDIES chalked where it says 'Gentlemen'.

\* \* \*

It begins at Abbotsbury, and moves
in white formation on mysterious

pumping wings past Burton Bradstock
towards Lyme Regis: a stretch

of the coast which I have not seen
since I was in a push-chair, 400 feet

by half a mile, a strip of land which
one Christmas Day (the beach bucking

and heaving) slipped and became a no-go
area – my first long distance path.

\* \* \*

Blue Pool you will remember
from your childhood, remember

how a suspension of magic dust
charmed the water to a turquoise

blue; but if you now believe
that a pit cut in the raw clay

with saw-edged conifers
can never be what those dreamy

primary moments want it to be,
then stay here by the sea, unjaded.

* * *

Like babies, pebbles all look alike
until they are wet, when their individual

way of calling attention to themselves
drags at the heart. One picks them up

lovingly, only to see a notice: *Removal
of any stone from this beach prohibited.*

Katie is in rapt innocence playing with
three I tore from the avaricious grip

of Fortuneswell and smuggled away
past Portland Prison: the thick end of the wedge.

* * *

The five paths that have been engraved
into the tilting cliff look like lines

on manuscript paper: gulls
are wild sharps that have escaped from

a Scottish jig. Last night, the three of us
were playing 'Sweet Lass of Richmond Hill',

and my fingers could barely scale
that height. Now it is these unpractised legs

that do the bowing – and I who reel
at another 'brisk and sprightly' zig-zag.

* * *

The arm of an old wooden signpost
lopped to shore up the path.

Tooled capitals catch the eye:
TO THE … then a row of

fossilized asterisks.
An underground protest song? Or

the opening of High Windows?
Some shelly skylark? 'To the place

where Thomas Hardy …' No. A glimpse
of the C says it all: CAR PARK.

\* \* \*

Black borders to the lobster pots:
a tarpaulin; some lengths of hempen

line; the odd claw; and a smell of
decaying wrack … this is the tide-mark

at Ringstead, where something once
tolled an entire community and

its livelihood to a few grassy mounds.
The man in the larch-lap hut collected

our money and said it was The Black Death.
The breakers repeat their plea of ignorance.

\* \* \*

There's nothing like the present, you said.
And at present we are being side-drummed

by the winds on top of Burning Cliff, where
not so many storms back lightning struck

the oil-shales and they smouldered
for six years. Nothing smoulders now.

We are blundering through a peace-time inferno,
blinded by so much wholesome air;

ack-ack from our anorak hoods
and shelter from a decaying pill-box.

* * *

There is a minor character in *Moonfleet*
called Greening: he had 'a singing voice

for all his drawl'. When Sir read it out
in English, we all smirked. Now they smirk

at Sir. He was a free-trader, of course,
and not a poet; though I too –

seeing a figure ahead of me on the path
who looks like a teacher – hide

my roughbook as if it were a tub of white
brandy, and hunch behind a blank face.

* * *

A fresh slipping away of the cliff-edge.
That garden's windbreak of pines

has been left with its roots flailing
like a beached jellyfish. The road

itself is under threat where the sign is
that says the cliffs are dangerous. A small

wooden shed fifty feet from all this
turns out to be the Church of St Catherine,

devoutly creosoted, the vicar's calling
card pinned to a wayward shingle.

* * *

A wreck flickers below the high tide
at the foot of the cliff; here on top,

old gun placements glare at Portland Harbour;
higher still, a helicopter whisks through

loose cloud; while at our feet
the stuff of painters' colour clings

to wet boots as we slither down towards
Osmington Mills where Constable once

honeymooned, measuring in creative peace
the golden mean of Weymouth Bay.

* * *

A Mediterranean blue raises its glass to us
from Poole Harbour as we pass by

in our woolly hats, Peter Storms,
scarves, gloves, and mud-brown wellingtons.

The white sails tilt and tack with balletic ease.
We plough straight down through the mud furrows

towards the promontory. The sea sighs 'Martini'.
We stop for a doughnut and a hot decaff

with a couple who have left Britain
for the coast of Spain: Old Harry and his wife.

* * *

'We have given up our homes where we lived
for generations to help with the war

to keep men free': and now we are free
to go to any other part of the Dorset coast

but Tyneham village where that notice
is yellowing on the church door. Approach

with your handful of Kimmeridge Coal Money
and make your offering to the guards

who haunt this ground. There is danger
from unexploded myths. Go carefully.

* * *

In Winfrith churchyard, a tibia,
a radius, two phalanges, a split flint,

and a rusted sickle blade are gathered
under a yew tree; on Winfrith Heath,

the Atomic Energy Establishment's
Steam Generating Heavy Water Reactor

and its twin cooling talismans try
to cool the word which the wind

keeps bringing from the east –
that word, and dust from tumuli.

* * *

The Japanese flash-guns keen.
Corfe Castle – an exposed

breadth of ashlar bastion,
which all the explosives the past

could muster couldn't smash.
But the day we run from the flash

over Bovington Camp, which
of our many towers will prove

indestructible? What dropped
Olympus lodge in the Purbeck clay?

* * *

There were two things worth photographing
in Tolpuddle: one was, of course,

the great pollard – condemned to its sixth
life sentence of steel bands and cement,

in exile from anything remotely sycamore-like,
the bulging belly of a Giles caricature;

and the other – quite unexpectedly – as we
left the green and passed the Martyrs' Museum,

was a thatcher, smiling down on us from the blue,
clutching at straws, and oblivious of the irony.

* * *

Katie was sucking noisily at the breast
as we said a last goodbye.

Now you are halfway back to
the Midlands and your decision whether

to pay two thousand pounds for an
'in vitro'. We are still here,

the Cerne Abbas Giant thrusting his
two thousand years of potency at our

parked car, as I try to catch
thoughts that spin like sycamore blades.

*Easter 1987*

## START POINT AT DAY'S END

For her, everything blows fresh, whether
it's a dull sea mist, the days a no-through
tunnel of grey and rain and megalith

seas forecast; or whether we all melt
like wax effigies in the prickly spells
of July. Whatever, for her mother and me

there was a staleness until this crisp light
and breeze came with late afternoon, tension
unfolding in little receding wrinkles.

Seagulls sit on benches outside the pub.
No shrieking, not even that hubble of
the machine that pays out pebbles, as a

barmaid, beautiful seawitch or mermaid,
emerges from the weed and smoke to bring us
foaming bitters and coffee like oil.

A small smack here at anchor makes
the sound of one hand clapping. Another
is laying pots like peacetime mines.

Motors that have tightened garottes around
Bolt Head have been unchained, escorted
back to lock-ups, their accomplices left

to dry out on the shingle. On the cliffs
one sober walker has walked into a cloud
of red that he tells himself are moths

hatched for sunset. No sunset yet: though
the tide is far out, and the Start Point keeper
believes – poised, white – it's high time,

so pushes this evening our three-year-old
swings on, high above the foreshore, towards
a half moon that's half come or half gone.

# FOTHERINGHAY

## (1989)

*While with an eye made quiet by the power*
*Of harmony and the deep power of joy,*
*We see into the life of things.*

Wordsworth

# FOTHERINGHAY

Fragments of what England
used to be, tucked
in corners of September:

a park, with its oaks
like a dining room in
a stately home, thrown

open to the public, but
cordoned to keep the sheep
and their deep-pile

instincts, their appetites,
their Sunday cries of
*ah!* and *ah!* from coming

to the table. Turf
reseeded, so we may
browse where we belong.

*

Who keeps doves now? In
Eaglethorpe – where a girl,
out jogging, flusters

past me into the woods – is
a perfect dovecote. Not
just for good luck, but

to feed the golden manners
of the Lord in his great eyrie;
squabs, white as her breath-

lessness, feel the knife
pierce them to the board,
know his hidden talons.

*

Sheep rise, and there is a
ripple across the sky, as if
the master of its domain

with his four-wheel drive
had printed a snakeback
cirrus track, and then appeared,

making his broadcast, hands
in a nitrates bag, redeployed,
bright yellow, full of the day.

\*

Past preaching doves, towards
a steady tolling bell,
calling the congregations

that are gone. A water-
meadow comes to feel
precious on such a morning.

A man could be a divining Y
held by the earth, and I
a jay-walker between spires.

\*

The way is not direct
to that eight-sided crown,
but through a web, a zig-

zag of scaffolded planking
across the dry ducts of
a flood-plain that knows only

guttural until February.
A sluice gate hangs like
a guillotine. Poplars press

to watch the matronym on a
pleasure craft descend into
the cold print of a lock.

\*

The weir race holds forth
through all mere prattling
and there is no barrier

to stop a child falling.
*No Fishing*, the sign says,
but the footpath casts

towards brown eddies where
these meadows end and the church
vane is a spinning lure.

\*

A lantern tower to guide
huntsmen home through
Rockingham Forest, which no

visitor finds, except in
his mind, meandering
between bare fields towards

where the boar first
charged, and the red
deer lay down her false

antlers. A man in shirt-
sleeves, a camera slung
around him, leaps a stile.

The light is perfect for
a photograph of the
castle that is not there.

\*

Soliloquize – don't
hurry along this green
lane, there is too much

history to be plotted.
This does not feel like
paths you have walked

on other Sundays, nor is it
because you are escaping
tensions at home, your new-

born nephew in the house,
his birthday forever
September; no, it is

the enormity of this small
hamlet you have so long
procrastinated in reaching.

*

How our own expectations
surprise us: the mound
where I had imagined

I would imagine Mary
Queen of Scots' last
toss of the head and

thread of Latin, Richard
the Third's first loss and
Yorkish howl, is today

common ground, a flag
with 'Caravan Club'
jauntily planted on the site

of the block, and a tartaned
weekender boorishly
munching bacon in the sun.

*

Overlooking a smell of
black plasticky hay
and molasses, in a loop

of the Nene, the motte
seethes like a forgotten
corpse. September's end,

and hotter than it should be,
as if the world were just
beginning to sweat at

some of the past wrongs
only now it's old enough
to feel and regret.

*

Twin toddlers slide
down the path from
the keep; a man

and a woman restrain
an Alsatian. I inspect
two plaques on a fence

interning one fragment
of a refuge. The river
curves irretrievably.

*

Nowhere to sit without
getting pricked or stung
to watch a power-

cruiser pass, or listen
to that robin try
to voice past freezings.

*

No day is adequate,
no life, to take in
what this hand's-breadth

offers up: but only to sit
like a stylite on one
high moment, is as much

profundity as a Sunday
in a working week
will allow, or the rev-

rev of a congregation
reversing past holes
in the sky, or the boring

pneumatic noises
people make – civil
teachers and engineers.

*

The church has a sign
on the door warning me
no valuables are inside.

Instead, everything is
out for harvest: a glazed
plait on the altar, pears,

pumpkins, marrows, eggs,
love-apples great and small;
along with the jars of

yellow pickly heat and rape-
flower honey … No valuables.
All is empty, secure.

*

Fotheringhay brings
home to me these natural
thoughts from the richest

soils of England. One
native pine and a hump
of briar are the last

flickerings of sleeping
booty; now autumn is
no longer rusty witchlocks,

but sun kisses earth from
open skies where hair
rises a manchet white.

\*

The plea a village pond
makes when it's frozen
and a beer can strikes,

the sound of everyday
returning, the freezing
over of whatever warm

song came streaming today:
those trusty paratroopers
up in the trees palisading

the church – the rooks – pick
at Midland clay as if they
hoped to resurrect a forest.

\*

A parachutist has been
released from a small
private cross, to become

micropolyphony: a whelk,
a periwinkle, in the blue
Sunday tides; it drifts

his/her hazy way down
with another and now
others like seeds from some

vanished theme, which yet soars
over the church, a falcon
freed of its fetterlock.

\*

Days like this are not
given for nothing: they are
to highlight the new

haws formed in the hedges,
to focus a three-months
blur in the sky on

what matters, to teach us
to distinguish between the
grey rippling of the ash

and the torrential log-jam
of wedges in an oak. It is
to make us notice that

motionless white-tailed wind-
pump, and look up to
the hum of aerobatics.

\*

Days like this are of a
glass that you can look
through and see other days.

*September, 1989*

# HUNTS
*Eclogues, Nocturnes, Elegies*
(1989, 1999, 2009)

## *Huntingdonshire Eclogues*                                    *1989*

Here it begins, with the rains of December
that emboss our new north-facing panes and play tom-tom
on the polythene skin across our porch footings.

Like a breath of the primeval: savagely alone,
confronting the spray from Kinder Downfall, or
New Year's Eve paralytic among the Trafalgar Square

fountains ... Just negative ions, I suppose, making
the stone lions whimper in the subterranean passageways
of my past. *Past!* our broken guttering echoes.

The water table must have been steadily rising all today –
a thought as cold as quicksilver threading a glass capillary.
The earth mother has lowered her pendulous warm front,

to lean so close above the bed where her water babies lie
that we may be cut off by our own daughter's bed-time.
Darkness is rolling in and the builders have all gone home.

They built the house across the lane on the site of a pond,
our neighbour tells us, and laughs at the thought that one day
it will inseminate that city couple's barren double brick.

Behind them, a single field of darkness stretches hedgelessly
towards the Great Ouse. Our 'common stream', as brown
as a common hare, hides in its form there. It has been known

to close the A45. No traffic down the lane tonight,
except a pig-farmer's tractor trundling autumn slurry
away to spread, great wheels scattering pearls of muck.

*

The soil is just solid clay. I watched a man
outside our local do-it-yourself store turning a wedge
left by the developers, and he looked like a

lone yachtsman ruddering the Atlantic – tarry
crests clung to his spade, his soles, and would not
grant him a moment's leisure. I have attempted

to walk some of the rights of way, have followed them
beyond the public footpointers, tracking their red
dotted tails to earth; but soon my legs felt as heavy

as a dismounted crusader. After the long rains,
a short stroll between the barbed wire fences of a barley field
can be like a spell on the Somme; and if you meet the ploughs,

they are Wellsian war machines, scarifying the landscape
to a nitrogen cloud. I always keep my head down
and search for little artefacts of peace, but have only ever

found pitiful fragments of a willow pattern tea-set
between the JCB-smashed concrete chunks of runway
where Americans set out on their bombing raids. My neighbour,

born into an expendable shire, into a house
long drowned beneath a reservoir, has a collection of
black discs picked from behind his plough-team. Their jingle

is more of a bony click. He lacks the cash it would take
to build a downstairs extension for his wife with her bad hips:
*Wouldn't need no foundations, of course. That's solid clay.*

*

The well beyond our double glazing is not from a garden centre,
nor a book of nursery rhymes: no gabled roof, no winch and pail
on a noose's length of nostalgia. Not a well you have to

throw dollar bits into before you can draw up a dream. This well,
where we have imagined our new patio, is quite invisible, and capped
by stereo concrete slabs it would take Wagner's Fafner and Fasolt

to shift. A tub, a trellis, and a thick variegated mass
of creeping evergreen conceal it; and the larch-blade dividing our
property from our neighbour's (Jill to my Jack) bisects it.

In the Chilterns there is the Maharajah's triumphant Victorian bore.
In Derbyshire there are the summer carnival frames of clay and petal.
But this humble inbetween well is a memorial to a late absence

of mains water in Huntingdonshire, when the inhabitants of Stonely
and this row of terraced estate cottages (each one extended now,
each quite separate) came together every morning to receive their dark

benediction from the earth. How did they all live? I know one was
a gamekeeper who would hang his Sunday rabbit inside the well
to keep it fresh, while sixteen feet below him the unidentifiable

ancient coin glimmered enticingly. I have never looked into
this hole we own; but when Mr Corp, our builder, suggested we might
have to fill it in, his Welsh draughtsman brought a magic wand and,

as my wife held Katie back, the slabs slid clear for a moment:
a cool smooth-sided tunnel down through the years' alluvium,
through the clay left by the ice sheets. She wished I had been there.

*

Poets live between their sheets of A4; but bricks are the thing
for ordinary mortals. Was it your great-grandfather, Stuart, lived
for a while in a 'Brickyard Cottage'? Now, having lain low

and watched the streetlamps creep closer and closer to your den,
you will do the same. Those stars you couldn't have borne to see
blanked out have guided you here where clay was cut and moulded.

Cover was all you wanted, and spotting across bare field rims
one small shabby copse and a house, you thought: a clean sheet.
Let those old mattresses, prams, abandoned fertilizer drums

stay hidden within the pit within the copse. 'Sign here!'
your width-of-a-combine road whispered, and here – the arc-lights
of Molesworth on the horizon – you are. HERE THE POET HENSON

LIVED FROM 1987– not, I'm sure, like another Sir Walter Scott
potboiling his life dry to pay for the bricks. Nor even a Yeats
locked in that Tower, one skew-whiff ladder up to the arrow-slit.

But breathing pure John Clare; sweet verses of open air.
Nothing could confine such an image maker, until the very
hedgerows became the walls of his asylum … Blue plaques?

Two peacocks were all that awaited us on the far side
of the ditch the day I helped you move in. You have decided
to adopt them, feed them. And, since a Shell Guide tells me

peacocks – according to Christian myth – are an assurance
of immortality, you were wise to christen yours so quickly:
Antony and Cleopatra. Perhaps Shakespeare was a peacock lover.

*

March, and already the winds prove it. The *Hunts Post* tells me
the mad March hare can be seen in the open field these days,
boxing or lying low; but I have yet to see one. Wind

is all I have seen, or the effects of wind: one larchlap panel
in our fence had loosened and soon the boundary line was snaking
wildly in the clay; so today a man has come with a steel rule.

The wind unnerves me. I cannot settle to anything. Instead
of putting coherent words on the page, I find my eye is drawn to
movement in the lane: green fairy wands, and winsome ragged skirts

of my neighbour's weeping willow, or my ear is hooked on the squeaky
drag of insulated cable where it coils into my study and my computer.
Then zephyrs from the window touch, like an aeolian harp, that map

of the Stonely enclosures: each strip becomes a string that sounds
an aleatory life: *Mary Hemmings Lands, Jona.Cuthberts Lands,
Geo.Rusts Lands*; there *The Orchard*, here *Great Meadow*, and where

our garden ends, the inscription *Hare Close*. The thought of a hare
concealed in that post-war enlargement, in that blank exposure,
where two dozen families scraped an anonymous living, is as chilling

as today's wind. Hares were thought to be witches' moon-creatures,
symbols of increase and of long life; seek them in stone-age caves,
Egyptian tombs; they're as elusive as fire; the hieroglyphic hare says

*Exist.* It suits the hare that our hedges have gone, it leaves
his ballroom free: one sunrise you may glimpse two dozen waiting
in a solemn circle; or at sunset hear one cry out like a child.

*

He set crocuses and daffodils along Old Ford Lane
for others' pleasure. That we had noticed and admired them
pleased him immensely. As public, as rough-hewn, and original

as that concrete heart he laid before his sleepy wife one
St Valentine's morning, and which still hangs beside the elm
stumps, impervious to disease. There was nobody else

we knew who would throw back their window and call from
dinner – *Have a claret!* – or *carrot* as I once misheard,
imagining some avuncular party trick ... His generosity

was a magician's black box. One evening, we returned home
beneath a vast umbrella of fresh rhubarb: eaten, it set the date
for our daughter's birth. The day David Llewellin died,

there had been unlooked-for perturbations in nature, the kind
bards exaggerate when a great man has fallen, the kind
Glendower boasted for his own nativity (*Signs have marked*

*me extraordinary*). When we tried, your last weekend,
to visit Spring Cottage, we found the skeletal footbridge
washed by a new ford; what had seemed a senescent trickle

become a lethal tide. By the time six days had carried
that week to its end, the waters had subsided, one willow
shattered, the rest of the lane swept grey. Now, today

as I push our daughter across your bridge, the Kym lies
peacefully retired; and in the uncut verges, crocuses
give way to daffodils, St Valentine to Persephone.

*

Leaving the garden centre, I find myself tugged towards the river
by an invisible line. Struck by its cool unruffled progress
in spite of the thick electric air of this April afternoon,

and following the path – across a lock, beside a fresh willow
plantation, away from the cars and fancy barges for hire –
I thought of you, Chris, whom this landscape could never quite

inspire: your attempts to capture it were always like today's
grey thundery sky, something was choking to get out.
And I chastised you for not putting enough of the 1980s

into your art. Painting, like poetry, must contain news,
I pronounced. So when you unrolled the landscape east from here,
and you'd left in, like the shape of a missing penny stamp,

Barford Power Station, I would have approved, had a poet
born just below it, who thinks the works of Shakespeare and Rowe
more powerful than anything our high tension age has strung,

not sung: *Paint water meadows, paint the Golden Age!* Chris,
you've gone down to another county now, to one more classical –
villas, august downs. On our prosaic bypass, heavy

laureates thunder towards their metropolis. My footpath leads
beneath such, through a mesh of hawthorn where high voltage
lines converge. Here I try to transform those cooling towers

to what I had hoped you'd see – a huge and concrete henge
where mysteries that we have switched off for our palmy Spring
hibernate, and the Great Ouse curves knowingly past.

*

This morning's fierce debate (Mrs Thatcher and the Police State)
has calmed to thatched cottages and a faint aroma of pig …
Our friends, who have battered themselves all year on the tubes

and against the bars of suburban London, have come here to recover
beneath these oaks. I walk them to the Stately Home and back;
but when our neighbour's trap comes clop-clopping through the mist,

they double-glaze: a clip from a Dickens film on *Breakfast Time*.
Nor will they believe that our newsagent closes today. I explain
you cannot change things too suddenly: he had those same blinds

down when a stray bomb blew news of the war on to the cobbles.
People like their Sundays left, their pram-resistant pavement
kept as it was, along with those ghetto-blasting church-bells:

even the Co-op has to dress up in Gothic script ... No, they will
never need the riot shields in Kimbolton. Cenebald knew a safe seat
when he saw one. And what would anyone want to change? Except

those few who, in scattered yet-to-be-modernised cottages (usurped
horse-kings, forgotten drovers, pleachers of hawthorn, hollers
of clay), do without double garages and swimming pools ... This year two

such originals died: their names I never heard ... The developers',
the builders' names, the names on the cherished number-plates –
these I can't help but know. The lanes swarm with prospective buyers

out for a spin – seeds from a tough fast-growing urban species.
Though all that ever seems to germinate is leylandii: quick-
hedging that looks like the artificial grass they drape at burials.

*

Widescreen, to *Gone with the Wind* themes, the Spaldwick road
slow-pans you towards forgotten footage. You spot the odd barn,
a token hawthorn butt, and countless anonymous farm-tracks –

but the tracks are too straight, harder than they need be.
Each barn, as you make your approach, becomes a corrugated hut.
The road unreels its title sequence but your senses are enmeshed

by the foulness of brussels, silage, or is it that dead hare
you swerved to avoid? You do not expect to find living things out here.
No house for miles and, apart from the bird scarers, bird-noise

would be the only sound if you were to wind down the glass: peewits'
low-level, high-volume aerobatics, or the viffing of skylarks –
like two half-witted, crack-voiced veterans of the old hundred:

make a joyful noise unto the Lord of Air-space! And so it fell
that half a century ago Dwight Eisenhower sowed the bulldog's teeth.
But there was no Golden Fleece; only, somewhere over the rainbow,

the Rhine ablaze. Now, occasionally, in the summer, a coachload
of balding shades will pause on its way to the Madingley graves to hear
that this is the village where Clark Gable's suits were tailored

and none will be told the uncanny tale that the village keeps and
does not advertise: the local man who was up and out early jogging
the broken runways, who saw what he saw, which is said to have been –

but secrets are what the Spaldwick road keeps best: the mist
encloses them more surely than the perimeter wire seals Molesworth's lips.
Unnumbered aircrew must have left from here. Some perhaps returned.

*

A straight grassy track, broad as a road, yet not made up –
only for Delius lovers, Vaughan Williams drovers –
a bridleway which unzips the fantasy realm of rape, splits

the cereal boxes on the table top, interrupts the unrolling
soap of everyday country farmside life, like a headline
that's truth and which can scarcely be believed amid so much

high yield fiction. I walk this straight grassy track trying
to ignore what surrounds me, the pollen-induced mirage
of fecundity that can find no need, so allows no room,

for skylark, hare's form, blue butterfly, or scattered poppies,
but will fuse in a core whole fields of sunflower, for
your breakfast. Dawn heightens Honeyhill Wood with its ad

glaze, the flattery of arc lights. Shooting has begun.
Not the gas-filled bird-scaring tube that I know to be bluff
and so pass at each field corner confidently, but shots

that smash clay, and send the black retrievers slavering.
Landrovers are parked and the colonels parade in camouflage,
pointing barrels towards the sky. This is a day of peace,

and this is what peace and prosperity entail: the rich,
unreal, utterly flat glory of a wide screen, which curves to
wrap around one's fears with illustrations of how lucky

we all are, forgetting occasionally to erase the odd
blemish from the past, such as this long green rural sentence
cut to such dips by four-wheel drivers that my foot slips.

\*

On the main road I follow to work, there is a noise like wax
in the ears. You can hear it most clearly on a Sunday, when no
juggernauts are heading for their container shrine; but in winter

it swells the rush hour, and on a Spring night it will make lovers
stir in their dark lay-by. I have visited the weirs at Offord Cluny
on a flood morning, and stood on the sluice-gates, and been stunned

by the sheer force in the hands of that one authority: a 125
crossing the crossing was all but drowned. And I watched the anglers
silent, cowled like Cluniac monks and a canoe and its paddle

hang cruciform in the race. But I did not imagine that our own
good brook (a dried up ditch for much of the year) could ever abraid
such excitement. Yet today, out of interest, I left the right of way

and followed its sluggish course for the quarter of a mile or so
it meanders around to Hellett's butcher's shop. The cereal crop
pressed close to its banks and there was brittle purpling elder,

ash-spears, scrawny umbellifer, and bath-brushes of teasel: enough
to put visitors off, the river all rags and bottles and bags, a geriatric
drugged asleep. Yet that gentle pumping sound, like the approach of

deafness, drew me round to a last bend and – yes – a secret weir,
walled and wheeled and with a swirling cochlea. How could I
not have walked here before? It would become a place of pilgrimage,

to bring poems and parents to and perhaps even see a kingfisher.
Although, to be honest, when a cloud passed and the vegetation shook,
it also seemed the perfect place to conceal some dreadful crime.

*

Where there is a space, they must always fill it
with an estate: this corner of the village was a rough
variety of meadows and hedgerowed paths. No use

to a soul, let alone an estate agent. So it is
to be sold and fifty-seven 'dwellings' are to be crammed
between a meander of the Kym and the cemetery wall. Trees

must come down. And where those ponies now ponder and muse,
bulldozers will bray. Thus it was, is, and ever shall be.
That cottage, soon to be lost in rapid fugues of scaffolding,

is where the village organist lives. Then next door,
the Nonconformist chapel … But that's already been converted,
a Fiat at the altar; and on the lawn, like a little fenced shrine,

someone's aviary, its flashes of a life overseas somehow
in tune with the notes inside me when I am moved to walk here.
Imagine them, all in black, that congregation of the Free Church,

trapped in its pews … It would be a kind of justice if they
had become this song and bright ceaseless activity. But that
would be a foreign, unchristian fate for them. So now on down

past the White Horse. These days, I'm afraid, I drink more
than I offer up. What I truly worship lies outside, beyond those
pre-fabs (coming down soon for another estate): familiar greening

woodland in its slow curve towards a ripening Northamptonshire.
Hell would not be to have lived forty years with mice and draughts
in such a shack; but to be rehoused where I could not see that view.

*


Dancing on a dozen pin-sharp church spires, or swung out across
a high-voltage safety net, Huntingdonshire's sky outshines
every one of its other acts. It is, after all, the only space

they can't infill. Its sketches for a Manhattan dreamscape
never get any further than the drawing board, although the US
Air Force, we hear, has plans it's trying to push through:

our daughter shrieks at us – *SKY!* – and she could mean sparrow
or cruise missile, all's one joy to her. She has inherited
her grandparents' war-steeped optimism. Retired to the north,

to the Peaks, my parents don't complain our Midlands are too flat
or too fat, but smile rosily: *All that sky* ... although my father's
vision grows cloudy, and even with his silver-rimmed bi-focals

newly prescribed, I know he would not find it easy to pick out those
far-off splinters of an ideal caught in theatrical striplight
where the stratus ends – Little Staughton, Pertenhall, and Keysoe –

spires which the youngsters, who come on Sundays bearing tripods
and spirit levels, use as levelling rods to measure out and extend
their stake in the Home Counties. Fools' Gold, of course, but so is

the Siren-song of the Peaks. Today, discontented with the flatlands
and forgetting my parents' *be appreciative* smile, I beheld what some
would not find it worthwhile turning from a theodolite to witness: the sun

blitzing through to create a brief downstreaming gold-capped
pyramid of rays. Such an experience is over in a second or two, but
contentment rises in its silent bubble and sounds the All Clear.

\*

Ten miles: past gravel pits, along the crevassed verges
of the A604, and then through a maze of tiny agricultural tracks.
I hardly knew where I was going. I had no torch, no map.

Fidelity led me into this strange county, dizzied by ring-
roads, dazzled by oncoming juggernauts, hooted at by dark owls.
No moon, no stars. The signposts pre-war and unreadable. If a car

loomed on an uninhabited stretch, I would jump into the ditch,
too embarrassed to be caught, fox-guilty, in those 1 a.m.
headlamps. I had been away on a foreign language course, and you

left to oversee our move into Huntingdonshire. That evening,
a killing silence on the phone: it was to do with desire, but
more with the need for conception. I sent flowers: the worst thing –

which only left me one last train, and no taxi fare. Huntingdon
to Kimbolton on foot: the neon ghost glow of rape, cash crop grown
for the seed, not the flower; fatigued brain turning fat King Henry

on its spit, who picked our new home as his first wife's prison, thought
he could put away love and let his lust roam. Overlooking that castle
where she pined, the bedroom where my own wife is a green haze. I hurry

through fields in which no feelings can be hidden. Even today,
our housebound and telephoneless neighbours seem to know about all the
separations and liaisons in Kimbolton. Only this morning, you had taken

flowers to thank them for babysitting and you came back full of …
but then they probably also know how after that mad sleepwalk
five years ago, I stood and threw gravel at your window, grovelling.

*

I have walked to the Warren and found there a horseshoe,
and wondered if it was truly a relic of the team-ploughing,
or just one lost by a cantering schoolgirl looking

for bridleways: and I have held it briefly like a quoit
half despising my short-lived impulse (hang it up
to catch good luck), half thrilled that I might be seeing

through its keyhole into an elm-trimmed whitethorn and
blacksmith Huntingdonshire, where our local farrier
hammered this same shoe fifty years ago, when my neighbour,

unlettered, unhurried, would have been standing watching
the sparks peal from the forge, then have followed his huge
plough horse out of the travus, over the field he had to till.

The field I cross to reach Warren Hill must have been
ten fields then: there's a machine with caterpillar treads
parked ready to eradicate these pocked strips of charred

stubble, burnt upon harvest. Respect for fire lives on –
the word in red illumination flashes as you slow down
and take the bend. Wieland is in hiding. There, where

mechanics work their deft magic on a Scandinavian combine,
and have hung one of their workshop's rusty horseshoes,
points to the earth; or in that tubular alarm calling

volunteers to out-of-control and wilful late summer
burnings: folk congregate, strangers pull over, as if
for a white wedding, and the air is specked with passion.

*

No Huntingdon White Horse, no feature carved by Grim
or dropped by the Devil, no Tor where Alfred or Arthur might
have sat, no headless pack of hounds, no Dragon –

but a solitary antlered figure that seems to have leapt
from a Palaeolithic cave wall in France, prancing
across the eastern English landscape like a hobby-horse,

to the steps of a dance that has even inspired the wind
to a composition, and which it has sketched in starlings
on the horizon: *Oss, oss, wee oss!* it sings to itself

at winter sunset. Or when the stubble burning is in progress,
it crackles and strides between the dying fires like
a druid wicker man. But on schoolday afternoons, it looks

a procession of bare facts through the classroom window:
the progress of power; Cromwell's Ironsides about to charge;
Queen Catherine's funeral cortège draping the county.

First dawn of the holidays, I was out walking through
one of those islands of scrub kept solely for the game
and saw a sudden flash that I took to be Roe or Fallow,

but as I moved to where it had been, it became a skeleton,
man-made and erect. There is nothing at all ghostly about
a pylon – grey folded arms, the sheen of gunmetal – yet

home, I lit at once our little stag-headed altar:
the images flickered comfortingly as I lay chained by
my imagination, a landscape barbed with the literal.

*

When you take your car up to Catworth Filling Station, the man who
drives you back – blue overalls, white hair, and the hint
of a stammer – tells you that he used to drive a steam engine,

tells you as he glides you down the B660 (Catworth is way off the
bus routes) about the unrivalled beauty of the run up from Peterborough
to the Peaks, but also of his special love for the local Kimbolton-

Kettering line: he points out the station – your oiled and tuned
Austin singing over the stone bridge – a glimpse of clean washing hung
outside the waiting room, an aerial on the signal box. A busy

station until the line was closed, pulled up with the ease I press
CUT on this word processor and watch a sentence of Dickensian length,
plushly syntaxed, its etymologies, its allusions, peel into limbo.

Nothing of the old straight track can be walked – still either
BRITISH RAIL KEEP OFF, or wheatfields – but from the road its
stigmata cross the pale-skinned landscape, green and luxuriant

like the long barrow of a forgotten king. Once I committed
two crimes: first by trespassing there, and then by uprooting from
the trackside a runner of *Rosa canina* for our private reserve.

Planted, it soon submitted its own plan for a network – branch-lines
in profusion. But the old man driving your freshly MOT'd Mini
A-reg does not mention names and so you do not ask him about Lord

Beeching, but talk of elms, hedgerows, meadowland … and wonder
what he might make of the computer terminology you are learning,
drafted late as he was into the service of the internal combustion engine.

*

At Gimber's End, there's to be no more truck with sugar beet.
Where a last few elms hang on and the temporary sign
says SLOW, JCBs clear unprofitability into a bank

and scoop out a clay pit. Not, as it happens, a building site.
Nor a stable tomb in which to dispose of the sun-god. Merely
a reservoir, stocked with trout, trimmed with false bulrushes.

Sixteen steps lead up towards this new setting for the sun:
and when my daughter climbs ahead of me and her glance back
cries that there are wonderful things, two swans, like sentinels

come drifting across the evening. And as I watch them,
a female silhouette appears, with a white vessel, haloed
by strange light from the west, on which I'm convinced

she's about to remark; or perhaps a word to the child. Then I
will say how good to see some enrichment of our landscape,
that of all beauty's elements, water is the most precious …

*Private property*'s all I catch from the mouthful she flings
lugging her plastic swill bucket up the steps. I flush
into the evening sky, and though I desire to keep the peace

by telling her that when I dug, coped with clay, the cost
of butyl, the span it might last before decay by sunlight,
how slowly it filled, how fast the fissiparous pond life spread …

instead, I begin to defend the right of way we've followed –
*How'd you like strangers cutting through your front garden?* –
stumbling back down as the swans are fed waste and privatized.

*

September: we had been expecting the frosts to move in,
but today it was suddenly warm and the sky a cerebral
ripple of stillness. I took Keats out to beat the bounds.

But we were prevented by a hand carrying a can half-
full of blackberries, by lips complaining that they aren't
plump like they used to be, men don't trim the hedges,

keep charge of the landscape like they used … Sharpening,
this keen slow gaze reduced me to a grey scythe stone,
pierced me with blue, a bitter blue, camouflaged in cheery

lengths of hedge-talk. He did not know me; he guessed
I must be a city boy because I stood on the bend, one heel
kicking LONDON 63 MILES. He was born here – before the war,

before the First War. And as he talks, I feel myself
rolling on moss and imagine this figure climbing the years
always between persistent green flares of elm, upright,

looking for ripe fruit. He points to where men have failed –
a trench neglected, some kind of outlet – and then at
the new half-timber home, winking – *Not had floods for a while –*

*they won't know what hits them* … And then I told him,
dislodging the stone from my tongue, of old Mossie next door,
and the shift in his tanned smile was not so much shock

as a jerk to avoid another acorn. I did not open my small volume
after that, but walked the rutted clay around the back
of the village, past the allotments, towards the primary school.

*

Our village alchemist, high priest, who crowned
the Queen's Silver Jubilee with ore and set
Cleopatra's Needle in gems from his richest barge,

who rose through ecstasies to the top storey of
the Shell Building and exchanged jokes with the Duke
and various Princesses; our famous gunpowder Reverend

today sent nothing up into the sky; although he did try
with the revised version of the Book of Common Prayer
to lead us through the Valley of the Shadow, but the words

fizzed and went out. Then nothing happened. Spectators
wandering away. But we at last walked to where the cedar's
dark flames lick and spread, and there like an unexploded

ashbud he stood, glancing up into the wind, telling
the man with the spade that this was his first interment
in twenty-five years: all the others, he said, had been ...

but here comes the cortège: only the wife, the son, one
remaining cousin of this oldest original inhabitant ...
ploughman, it might have been said, worker for the duke, fire-

warden, school washer-up – as it might also have been said
he was content with his allotment, immaculate lawn, hedge,
had all words not been crushed by the bulldozers' *Little*

*bit of meadow and no peace.* The coffin is lowered,
and an arm like a black turnstile moves them on to dazzle
at the vacant grass, at a few brief extravagant cascades.

*

After we'd been last night to look for the ghosts of ridge
and furrow on the snow-trimmed fields at the end of the lane,
*The Winter Walk at Noon* was my bed-time reading.

This morning, the river that lay flat in the field's lap,
passive as Cowper's hare, has broken into a wild rush –
a rip hisses across the gravel track to Gimber's End.

My neighbour is out complaining about the lack of ditches:
*It's the council. These bloody houses. I don't care –*
*they can put up as many as they want now!* And stiffly,

futilely, sweeps the water from his gate. Strangers
are stopping to watch the pageant: the country's new regime.
Why did nobody predict that this sorceress would arise?

Range Rovers glide across the surface. Estate and Saloon
approach: bald heads in their glass islands pray.
Minis turn back to St Neots, to the saint of all Minis.

Noon is bright with the spirit of river nymphs:
the smallest hill looks the pap of a goddess. Reasonable
William Cowper keeps dropping words into my head as if to

dam these pagan emotions. *God made the country!* – but
my neighbour, who is dour and flat-voiced, replies
*It's more like a town, these days.* The *Independent* arrives,

and on the front page is a Huntingdonshire tragedy: a mother
dives to snatch her toddler from the floods, and drowns. The father
tries to rescue her; he also drowns. Only the child crawls out.

## HUNTINGDONSHIRE NOCTURNES                                          1999

Summer nights, they used to sleep out in the field,
these cottages get so hot: slate roof, no space
between ceiling and timbers: homes for a row of mere

husbandmen. To lie out looking up at the Plough,
at a night blazing cornflower and poppy, before electricity
sowed the village in its herbicidal shroud of light.

Even now, when – in our shire or the next – there's lightning
and the dark snaps in, you are at once unwrapped to something
those who hop on their packages to the sun forget is here

under our feet. It earths. Like the fires that burned in the fields –
hateful to wildlife, but you felt the country was alive. As vile
as the fox-hunt, and as stirring, watching those red flames

hack through a crop, scorch a tree, sear hedges …
A far cry from the sober soul who came to read the meter,
resting his knee on the bed, mouthing dry numbers.

Last time the power went off, we got out the candles.
I talked of how my father used to go to bed
with a nightlight (and his treat of bread and milk) and gave one

to Rosie – in a jam-jar. Read to her. Left it at her bedside,
flickering on her wicker chair. *The Wicker Man* I think now –
that cult film I should not have seen when I was a boy.

She tried to move the jar, using three paper tissues,
because it was hot. The heat caught the tissues and they fell
like fire balloons on to the carpet. She called. I came

and smothered three small blazes with my bare hands,
just as they were reaching for her dress, her fairytales, the whole
tinderbox. I'm told we need cover: 'New for Old'.

*

At eleven minutes past the eleventh hour on the eleventh of August,
the moon – that just happens to fit across the sun
like a watch-glass over a watch – will just happen

to cover the sun once more. In Huntingdonshire, where we
are less demonstrative, where our hele stones are hidden deep
beneath a glacier-load of clay, our wishing-trees under peat,

we will not black out completely, but retain our self-control.
Rivers will roll on to the Wash. Traffic will move unmoved.
After all, it started here in the sixties: the first bite,

the fading light. For Baily's beads, the gravel workings.
For the diamond, a concrete shopping precinct. Where the corona
of a Cromwell or a Cowper might have glowed, a ring-road.

*

Street-lamps are a topic of hot debate in the parish council.
This does not bother the moths, or the youths who silhouette themselves
beneath, groping at time-switches. Nor does it interest

the owners of security lights that leap out bare-
toothed at the eyes of evening strollers, such as Pearl, who passes
every night in her shell of literary ornament. The beams

flick on as they might flick off if she were using psi.
But she walks by, good sense personified. Our nightly
white patrol against the blackness, against Old Shuck.

In the dark, Hatchet Lane becomes a drain for every fear
the night can pour. It is a Grimpen, where only ignis fatuus
knows the way, a treacherous channel whose marker buoys

bob and mock and wink. There are hidden shoals. There are wrecks.
That lantern there. This beacon. Look – a distress signal.
A man adrift in a Zodiac. A woman clutching a ring.

*

Neighbour stalks neighbour. Honey fungus, rampant as the plague
in the middle ages. One comes home to startle him truffling
with the woman she thought was a friend. Another puts out feelers

and finds it on the grapevine. Seedless. Sour. Nocturnal
diversion for the middle classes. White-knuckle distraction
from the sound of a siren wailing between the elm stumps,

across tubercles where hedges were, through the damp gap
and mound where a barn has fallen. Harvest festival of sex.
A casting out of clay and flatness, honouring tumescence

at ski-slope altars, in Dolomites of white flesh and
hard sweet paps that are not Papworth Everard,
Papworth Village Settlement, Papworth Heart Unit …

Traffic makes the pace and bypass leads to bypass.
Villages divorced from towns. Neighbour transplanting neighbour.
Pigs and partners cry for what has been taken from them.

\*

Too much cancer in the village. Too many lights on
after midnight, windows where desolate women stare
out across the furrowed days, a harvest come

although the summer has hardly begun. Such a yield
and such a loss. Every field's rich head of growth
stripped by chemicals. Every indirect path, the ones

that do not lead to the church, ploughed out, to plant
more dense grain. Too much that's systemic in our lane.
The averted gaze, the avoided subject, the 'putting out

to pasture' when there is only a stall and a machine. Human
kindness all silver topped. Rich local vintages
in obsolete skins. This village is too old. Too much has gone.

In the small hours, I look at the old map of the High Street.
*Crown, White Lion, Old Sun, Saddle, New Sun, George,*
*Fox, Half Moon* … and I think of all we've lost

in our late twentieth-century milk-round. Here he comes
again, moonlighting, opening the gate quietly. We swallow it
for our bones' sake. Too much cancer in the village. Good health.

\*

Huntingdon Life Sciences is expanding. The tests they do
on Ursa Minor progress to Ursa Major. Orion
looks to his belt of blue and prepares a knock-out dart.

The county is wearing its white coat to impress on us
this universal cold necessity: these little glass bottles,
icicles in a glacial advance. The night of science is windless.

Across the Fens comes the barking. From dark roads
cats' eyes gleam. On either side there are lethal
incisions, dykes like man-traps. Now here come the rabbits.

\*

One glimpse and a night of worry. While I was at
the Prom, listening to Poul Ruders' *Gong* – deafening
evocation of the sun – you were afraid we'd all go blind,

imagining next morning the plaintive words 'Mummy, why is it
all so dark?' Well, it happens, no doubt. Four hundred
calls to Moorfields Eye Hospital today. But yesterday

it was just a case of jiggling the A4 sheet to catch
that black smirk from the skies. The children watch the temperature
drop, the atmosphere turn grey and chill. We follow

the instructions (except for that quick glance up through the clouds)
because we believe in scientific advice. We don't believe
in dragons, we don't believe in omens or coincidences,

though at the very moment of totality, my mother in Scotland
finds herself talking to a stranger who is waiting to be picked up
by her daughter, her daughter who happens to live next door to us,

in that house half-painted white, where the shadow is smiling.

*

The medium tells Jane that her mother is with her on all
her car journeys, that there's something rattling in the boot (which
there is), that one of the doors doesn't work (which

it doesn't) and 'she doesn't like it when you pass the gibbet'.
This must be Caxton, just beyond the border
out of Huntingdonshire – *Toseland Yelling Graveley*

the sign says, like a lost line from 'Jabberwocky' –
there it stands, the gibbet, next to a Chinese Restaurant
and nothing else. A string of stories. Sheep-stealers. Spinsters.

A woman wouldn't want to break down there, as I did.
No shelter, no hedges or banks, and only one tree.
A Knight of the Road arrived, with his own private gallows.

*

Where the great bough fell from the ash last week, a cuckoo pint
is sprouting, its clustered beads of scarlet, the last blush
of what its Lords and Ladies have been up to in the hedge.

It's the edge of an old settlement. Ridge-and-furrow as clear
as a baby's fontanelle. I so often tell our children what it means
they make fun as we walk home through feudalism's graveyard

skirting the glasshouse millionaire, the paddock where he keeps, behind
a newly painted ranch fence and electric wire,
two seaside donkeys. It is a path as solitary as that braying

for a lost beach. I tell my eldest not to walk it,
nervous of what is hanging out there, smoking, buzzing.
She's vulnerable in her purple blazer, striped and starched to the roots

and too deep in her Biology revision of spathe and spadix
to notice poisonous berries that have suddenly appeared beneath
her world tree, like an unpropitiated many-breasted goddess.

*

Then there was the night Katie stood out on the lawn
and watched the Leonids – twenty-seven, I think, she saw
shooting across her vision. We fumble with contact lenses,

the world shifts through our bi-focals, but she has seen
stars falling out of her childhood. And now she must learn
at school about the First World War. Her great-grandfather

on the Somme, watching the Very Lights, at that end
of this woodbine century. Tonight she has to pick out the fixed
points on a time line: pin-pricks like Kitchener, the Kaiser.

*

Is there a gauge in San Francisco to measure the effects
of acid rain in Huntingdonshire? I'm told there is a seismograph
at Tilbrook Grange that's monitoring the San Andreas Fault!

Not earthquake territory, you'd have thought. Though once I was sitting
silent, pharaoh-like, a hand on each rest of my armchair,
when I felt what I thought was a gust of wind lifting the carpet,

except that the air was still and the carpet stapled down.
The epicentre, I found out later, was in Peterborough.
Tsunami, volcano, forest fire cross our screen

night after night, while here the sea yawns, and puts in
its annual claim for Whittlesey Mere. But we live where
safety helmets are mandatory for a spin round Grafham Water,

past the tons of chlorine in the water treatment works,
into the woods where they found a hoard of mustard gas,
across the stable clay, ideal for disposing of plutonium.

*

The convoys – we never met one, but our friends did, returning
across the wolds near Leighton, turning up past *The Fox*
between the last elms into Catworth, they would suddenly meet

Grendel and Grendel's mother. This was when the name of Molesworth
rang as loud as Greenham. When the local shops put up
NO PEACE CAMPERS warnings and one could infuriate

blues with a simple litmus test. This was when 'cruise'
rowdily crossed the line from quoits on the sun-deck to
concrete shelters, fission of calculated mass. I knew

a man who helped design cruise missiles. He lived
miles from Hunts or Berks – but for us, those nights we tried
to conceive a child were patrolled by fear of the inconceivable –

our homes were Hrothgar's hall, our dreams a pack of floodlit
chase scenes from Spielberg. A politician comes to praise
the silos, posturing in his camouflage, hinting through oily persiflage

how vital it is to crush this dangerous but small minority,
these spongers, peaceniks, these rent-a-terrorist, women's lib
gay anti-family animal rights types

clogging our moral high streets with their camper vans.

*

Fireworks this village is famous for. They come for miles to witness
the Reverend's all-star variety performance, where the judge
once lived who sentenced Guy Fawkes to death.

Catholicism broods here, like the one that wouldn't go off, lurking
in its priest-hole, its side-alley churches. Even our spire flares
a Roman Candle to guide us, as it guided the B-17s

back from their attacks on V2 launch sites, or bombing
a ball-bearing factory. Remember the war. The blackout.
The bagatelle-board rumble from Warren Hill. And then the formations …

I met the heir to the fireworks empire at the post-office counter.
He's in the Territorials. Expecting to be called up
to Kosovo quite soon. Bomb disposal. Once November

and the Millennium are safely over, he'll be out there, clearing
mines and reminding us that war can never be cleared, however
we celebrate our VEs and our VJs with elaborate triumphant displays,

keeping his eyes on the ground, on the patterns the soil makes.

*

The caravans begin to gather on the green outside Kimbolton
weeks before the date. The Statute fair has come
round again, and our medieval village honours its eighth

century of trade – in men, in stock, and now in leisure.
St Audrey watches from the Fens as her one gift to the language
is unvoiced from every noisy pitch, each loser's

prize (for every child must win today) doled out
by wretched souls who show not a glimmer of that fun they hurl
as hatred at the world. Take your inflatable hammer, or your stuffed

blue whale. The Stattie Fair. Its hatebeat can be heard
across the parish. Its tawdry colours spout out of tradition's
trench like Very lights. We cannot hear ourselves

but fix a grin and load a stick with sugar spinning
like our sweet spun brains within our skulls, watching
those kids up on the waltzer. Adam in his gatehouse grimaces

but Vanbrugh knows this is the Restoration spirit.
Forget what passed within these houses during the Commonwealth.
Forget the witch-hunts and the families divided: bite your toffee-apple,

buy your token for the dodgems, and bump your brother, bump
your neighbour, but don't ask their religion, or whether they believe
in monarchs, or if the shops in Huntingdon should open on Sunday.

*

*for J*

At her age, you were packed off to Lushoto, to boarding school.
Think of that seven-year-old (as this one climbs the stairs to bed)
stepping up to wave from her Dakota – at Zanzibar, at her parents

who had an empire to run. Think of that childhood until then
on the mild clear Indian Ocean, shiftless, shoeless,
treading the red-hot corals, a bush-baby

clambering out of your dreams, and once a black mamba,
your ayah squatting, pounding a coconut. Think of the nights
the whooping woke you, your father bouncing you in his jeep

down the potted rutted roads, between elephants
and sleeping lions, in and out of giraffes, around
the waterholes and their all-night parties, observing

the moment the moon would show and Ramadan begin,
revolution come and send you flying into a black-and-white
heirloom of the toppled Sultan. Your childhood was Coral Island,

not Lord of the Flies, but hers … ? Born into the Heart
of Blueness, Little England, St Luke's Summer beer
and algaed reservoirs. No crescent of breakers. No sundowners

on a verandah with the Great White Hunter. Just Cowper and his hares
in a gamekeeper's cottage on a school-teacher's salary,
where the Lion King comes down like a tabby cat

to open a nursery school. Now we are seven, think
what matters to a child. A bear in a cave of dreams
at the sacred breast. Call it Hunts. Call it Zanzibar.

\*

When Rosie started pressing the buttons on her Pocahontas game
as I was trying to follow *The Triumph of Time*, I threw it
across the room in a rage. And then I remembered the real

Jamestown, founded by Sir Edward Wingfield of the Priory
here in Stonely. A virgin land he entered on, like young
Birtwistle confronting class and music. Patentee, artist

established their colonies, raised defensive palings,
played the crusader, blew fanfares at the tribes who gathered
waving hatchets and whooping. One night at the Proms

I saw Pierre Boulez conduct from the autograph score,
turning its pages like huge leaves of a tobacco plant.
One day at the school I walked into a drama class

and heard the wail of *The Triumph of Time* and called out
to my friend, who was always there ... Fifteen years ago.
And the Prom must be twenty-five. 'Writing music is like

driving a car at night, you can only see the headlights
and get an idea of the landscape.' Stonely Priory's dissolution
clinging to the hill. The soprano sax singing its lament

in Hatchet Lane. My daughter looks daggers at me.
The procession passes: an elephant, an angel, the grim reaper.
Our American friends ring and ring: there is no answer.

*

They dance like paper cut-outs on a length of fishing line
across our windy county. The tail of a kite so high
it's almost out of sight, the cross of a man's agony

held by a child with his hands together on holy ground.
They dance – a tower, a spire; a porch, a flying buttress –
to the fantasia of an organ, to the thunder-repelling carillon

and they call to dance those who have forgotten what it means
to stop walking, stop running and skip, hop,
hornpipe to the music in the nave. If ever the wind drops,

what then? And already there is a change in the weather. One paper
cut-out is gone, another is torn, the kite itself is flying
erratically, the dance is uncertain, the music is played by old

arthritic fingers, there are bell-ropes hanging unused. Sing
your Shaker tunes, sing your Wesley anthems, sing, sing
hymns ancient and modern, for the child with his hands together,

for the children who will find the paper fragments littering the landscape,
make boats of them, make a treasure hunt of them, and not know
the secret in these crossed sticks, this fabric, the very wind.

*

Wind slices at the sashes and the double doors, it lashes
across the cricket pitch, it challenges the right of obedient
classical pillars and portico, with their aristocratic air

of calm, to loiter as they have for so many hundred years,
as if the old Duke hadn't fallen at the final
African debt, as if all the King's boots

hadn't kicked the parquet in their war effort, before
the castle was sold to fill with boys and their skittle alley
noise learning about the Rhine, Gibraltar, Ulster …

As all the Millennium's nines come up in a last fling
of showers, who is it cowers there at the marble fire,
beneath the self-denying, appeasing gaze of that Montagu,

that smiling regulator, who has an idea what Cromwell
is up to in Drogheda, who knows that only a length away
Aragon withered, the English rose, but who cannot say

what shadows are there before him, or why this late wind
should so chill with its lottery numbers his gilt frame?

*

One evening we went to look for willows on the Godmanchester Commons.
Tree Wardens, we were being led by the Tree Officer
for Huntingdonshire. Gravel territory, where time ran out and the gavel

gouged its crater in the earth, where Ouse quakes in its orbit.
We walked into the dark and found the poor old men
dying of neglect, unpollarded, valueless: crying out

to be made into baskets or chairs, ready to split themselves
in two with the weight of their own inheritance. Dictionaries whispering
over and over *withies, sallies, osiers* to the damp

meadowland and fragments of fen. As we looked, the Crack Willow
corpsed, the Weeping Willow sobbed and the Goat Willows
skipped towards a landfill site, sun fading on their silver

trailing leaves. I know a song of willow, and it is about
ambition and jealousy and ignorance, nothing to do with cricket
or baskets or ornamental lakes. These willows must be cut down

before they stand a chance of survival, as a leg must be
amputated on a diabetic poisoned by his own sweetness.
The phantom limbs of the Ouse rise up as we walk home.

                              *


*for SECH*

I wanted to mention the fact of the elm that, turning for home
from yours, rises at the bend like a church on a ley-line to point
*This way!* A Huntingdon elm, no doubt, and so resistant

but the one notable crown in this crop-headed landscape.
I have delivered a book of elegies by an Irish poet you like
and now it is growing dark. A magpie. A star. Follow

the elm's word – turn where the silhouette of a bull directs:
past a royal suite of velvet cattle; the silos
and washing steaming on the Kettering line, the restored station;

the restored pub, sign drily squeaking PRIVATE;
the London milestone memorialising late coaches and transported
words like 'turnpike'; the business park's anthology, its title

engraved *THE HEART OF STONE.* There is no stone in Huntingdonshire.
Only the gravel they dug out of your childhood riverbed
and a few erratics, etched with unmelting lines such as these.

## HUNTINGDONSHIRE ELEGIES                                    *2009*

The land dries. Cracks open amongst the stubble.
In the distance, there is a strawstack the size of an office block.
The radio mast, wanting to stir and dissolve this pastoral,

broadcasts its reminder: you are not in the Tate, late walkers,
though there could be a god, and there have been nymphs,
their underwear, look, on the hawthorn bleaching. Was it Bacchus

with his chariot drawn by pards? Our walk to the White Horse
marks the end of summer. Only one light across the field
towards the disused branch line: there, under his bushel, glows

Il Penseroso, when he's at home and not out here, lyrics
pushing from dust like seventeen syllable knotweed,
stanzas flocking, sonnets ripening, vine translating the bricks.

From that locust tree whose seeds I brought you and you planted
after a Black Forest holiday, we follow the middle way.
We want to survive, but we also want to be Dante

entering Huntingdonshire's dark wood. And although
you are radiating Italy and Rilke as we walk and you're sure
this is a new path, the right path, you must know

that last elm on the horizon is dying. No dragonflies are flying
as they were this time last year. No owl yet. No buzzard
so late, though you tell me they are to be seen there preying

on rabbits. But it is a hare starts up and wheels round
the field like the hand on a gameshow clockface; then stands
framed in the hedgegap, tonight's winner against the sun.

*

*in memory of Peter Smout*

At one time, all lines interlinked, and you could travel
from any hamlet to beyond Waverley. At our extinct station,
up Bustard Hill, where a new car rolls across gravel

and parks at its platform; where a sudden steam revival
proves to be sooty effluence of a straw processing unit
that's moved into the sidings; where the shade of a manned level

crossing is just a washing line – at one time, a pipeful
of vapour trail dreaming summer on to a Huntingdon elm
and hedgerow chessboard would have marked the adjectival

release of an English teacher into the village: one who was careful
to note *Satyridae* near the Manchester Arms and plovers
piping him over the airfield; one who would cover the novel

by Christmas, poetry through spring, so to save all
the drama for May and June. Imagine the departure of a thinking,
breathing engine down that branch line. Imagine its survival

through Beeching, under Thatcher, pulling weary arrivals
out of Hardy (oil-lamp and key; whistle and flag)
into the new age, under its bridges, through its tunnels

to a privatized single track terminus. Now see it unravel,
though it gleamed into the heart of the country on its principles,
though its sleepers were oak, points faultless, inviolable

its timetable, in the nerve centre no signal, no bell.

                              *

They are trimming the English elm at the farm, the one that leans
and reaches and begs to be spared. 'It's good to be alive,'
calls Farmer Oldways, who woke one morning to headlines

declaring his wife had come back from the dead. I wave
and aim for the second surviving elm, a mile down the bridleway
into the next county, where Farmer Grudgingly once drove

his pickup at us for trampling the grants on his nest-edge
(our last walk here before my mother died), and reach an invisible
tunnel Farmer Enlightenment thought he must exorcise and purge

of its dancing white magic. The place tries to hum the steps
but it's mute. Only two swans, letting their silent springs
run down across the ploughfield, the keep-out sign, the rape

will join these floaters in my vision; while the high warbling
larks, the lapwings' beep-and-sweep may distract from tinnitus
like digital toys above that Boys' Own castle drawbridge

Farmer Templar-Knights says he uncovered there, and burned.

*

Stonely is a still life as August approaches: the hanging
begonias glow amber and red on the edge of decay.
The cat ignores a manic thrush at her nose, under swinging

strands of crumbling himalayan musk. Already the birds
have vowed they'll leave music to the wasps, to breezes
in the ash tree's first dry minor keys, and to half-heard

falsettos out of Luton, into Stansted. There is a ticking in the hedge.
That vacuum you took apart: its canary yellow filter
rocks on the patio. Was there talk of ordering an oven, a fridge

before the offers close? Nobody moves from their green chairs.

*

A witty return from Waterloo on the 'Bed-Pan' line,
to the road that winds us through Ravensden, Bolnhurst, Keysoe, adjusting
our language, like our watches, our currency, back again,

paying homage to those who have said goodbye to all this
and started over. Negotiating one bend (the piano teacher's)
then another (where the motorcyclist died), we erase

the long, straight boulevards, the avenues lined with planes
(that also kill motorcyclists, vamping until they enter)
as if parsing an Anglo-Saxon riddle transcribed into lanes.

Thomas Tompion's precision, Admiral Byng's folly,
Bunyan at the crossways. A Bedfordshire patchwork of pride
and obsession, before the mast, under an oak, or on helium

fireballing out to Beauvais. And into our county of revolution,
where the Earl who led the fight against the first Charles
became Lord Chamberlain to the second, we find a solution:

no harsh directive, but compromise. What in passing resembles
a gibbet or guillotine is a pub sign for the King's Head or the Plough,
whose few shares are in clay. At the last bend, all that tumbles

from the back of the Banks' tractor is sugarbeet, while a call
to the empty road says something about hunting, and another
cries *God* or *Fête*. The milestones keep their distance from Whitehall.

*

*for Katie*

In Hunan, you stand before the thousand adolescent boys
who are going to take over our world. In Huntingdonshire, a heron lifts
from one brown square the frost has conceded, and flies

across to the priory fishponds. I think of the carp that have lurked
there no dynasty can dissolve, as a microlight brushes
its ideogram on the sky and moorhens squabble for space. I have worked

in this provincial outpost for a quarter of a century now, while you
have only taught through the first phase in China; but already
you're taking on the Terracotta Army, the Great Wall … We email you

daily – there will be texts and phone-calls. Even letters. And yet
distance is unscrolling still out of BC. When you were ill,
they dosed you with seaweed. You dine on frog soup. The people greet

your fabled size-seven footstep with a drumband and bouquets.
October declines; the five-yearly congress lingers on
in Beijing; and here the leaves turn yellow, shortening days

harden the unconscripted clay of our fields. Your mother mentions
something from Arthur Waley. I quote the *Tao Te Ching*. We send
our thoughts to you as far as Guilin, Yongzhou and Lanshan.

*

Past where we took our German friends last July
when they arrived late from Somerset and I made the mistake
of thinking I knew the way up that farm track to the B&B

at getting on for midnight, mists beginning to swirl,
our convoy crawling over a bare field until at a fork
shadows came rattling, and the territorial snarl

of dogs, gutturals, guns (or did I imagine that?): *Yirr at
the wraang place ...* today, I hurry on and into
a turning I have never taken, off Cage Lane, the light

uncanny, the sky a fractal scrim of autumnal liberties
as this unmarked, unnamed way winds up towards
an ash tree watch, its primal spears and gilded keys,

where only a 4x4, suspicious, blacked out, brakes
to let me approach the words HER MAJESTY'S PRISON,
as if they were a translation of time or loss or mistakes.

*

The airfields still surround us, populated by willow-herb and hard-core
with crumbling concrete lollipops that slip from the grasp, the limp
of a runway, a nodding HQ, up the skies to Bedfordshire. One swore

he encountered aircrew there on the anniversary of the crash.
Another recalls aligning himself in fog to our medieval spire.
Now here Glenn Miller slides us 'In the Mood' to the lash

of wind through wheat. A last performance at the Corn Exchange,
then wurlitzered into legend. Your mother had danced to him that week.
We walk around the old control tower, restored, arranged

to look as if the men are just next door, a jacket over
a chair back, an open map, ten Players or a pipe, the typewriter
with a weather report in it ... Eventually, no one will believe

so many lives were propagated, grew and flew and dropped
seeds of what we're lost in now, our high yield days
that close ranks over this unyielding, ineradicable crop.

*

Fog, the first of the season, blurs our garden's parallels
and frost graces the lawn, the rotary drier's web,
the plants that no one has dead-headed, old mountainbike wheels.

The weeping cherry planted for our silver wedding (and severed
straight after in a single act of negligence) is beginning
to reassert its habit over the tumbled green chairs of summer.

There is a glaze across the pond and our one fish, veteran
of the heron wars, is a hologram reminder of lost gold.
Ash keys hang unrattled; shrivelled hips and deep-veined

ivy hide the remains of an elder. The ladder is still
against the shed where we keep all that the children have outgrown,
where adolescence has mildewed magic, animal, doll

and picture book, where Christmases fade. The birch and apple
are like Gabriel and one of Scrooge's ghosts. There is a hosannah
and some humbug in the hedge as next-in-line saplings

wake from a recurring dream of being spears, of resisting
the villa and – that field our donkey brayed in twenty years –
the grove and lake and jetty, newly cut and pasted,

smiling in soft focus. Out of the gloom, a developer
fiddling on the roof, considers the best way of blocking
natural light, of draining time through plastic and fibre,

of keeping history out. But the climate has got there first,
with its impressionist demands. You can almost hear Monet
talking, driving a hard bargain and sealing it with mist.

*

Wind off the Easton Road from Stonely Priory blows
towards the castle where Queen Catherine is a pale flame
and every farmer, every labourer and lover, knows

what news it brings: it clings to them like keys on the ash
when all the flattering leaves are gone; the trees themselves
cannot conceal the operation: the soldiers flush

the priory well with poison, make a wafer of the door.
But in the darkness, the black canons have obediently
dissolved themselves into the shadowy perimeter

between their century and ours. A chant may be heard
in six high voices, unhooded from the suckering elms,
the new enclosures' layered thorn: a pattern of bird

migration and transubstantiation over Peterborough.

*

How does that wood pigeon manage to stay on the delicate
hair trigger tip of our silver birch, our world tree?
So self-importantly placed, so sleek and pompous and fat,

he ignores the small birds' clamour for grub or crust
or crumb but enjoys a good view of all the millionaires
of Huntingdonshire: each new house bigger than the last –

forever upsizing, like post-*glasnost* Russian dolls.
Wind from the Urals shivers birchwhite to a ghost
of black canons with fish ponds and cony holes

and lynchet strips of twenty pigeon-tempting acres
and darker potences of squabs in dreadful concentration.
But the century calls: take flight, an away break

to the park or any extravagant Fen-trotting journeys,
keeping an open-all-hours mini milk bar
in his personal crop, pecking at those of others to earn his

award of Pest Status. He keeps his head high
and applauds himself as he leaves, offering one leisurely
*coo!* to the rest of the world's thin, wavering cry.

\*

First, the tree, from Top Farm and always too tall.
It drops its needles the moment it's dragged across the step.
It leaves its resin about. It lights up in the hall,

collapses: a confusion of glass, glitter, doves and fairies.
Not many years old, but it knows about Christmas.
So does the holly, a single female and what she carries.

So does the mistletoe, hugging a sick lime in the park.
Every leylandii has been coiled into a wreath for December.
Bonsai, poinsettia, amaryllis and hyacinth greet the dark

centre of the year with their xenophilic candlepower.
One day the countryside makes alliance with a hoar.
The next it is clay and couch-grass. But homes flower

electricity. The wind farm over the hill rejoices,
its wings hum; the Siemens man brings a meter
and the air is cross-hatched with icon-trailing voices.

\*

Caught in the space between Christmas and New Year, idly
wondering about Huntingdonshire churches: who uses them now?
Are we even closer to the fulfilling of Larkin's prophecy?

When the man in the four-by-four attempted to winch off
the lightning conductor from Little Staughton spire for the copper,
was that the beginning of the final act? Iconoclasts move

beyond stained glass and altar screens: they strike
at Michelangelo's very finger and bring down the roof. We snub
the churches around us and they ignore us back; though, on my bike

before Christmas, I reached Little Gidding and found the chapel
unlocked: not a soul, the community gone, a page
of signatures and Eliot on the wall; a bell, no steeple –

nothing for thieves or lightning. But something as shocking
struck me as I put on my cycle clips again and rode
home to wrap up your present – that book by Richard Dawkins.

*

So, Frost, what do *bad* fences make? Having just
left one so rattlingly ungainly, a poulter's measure
of a line without craft or gift or design, you'd not trust

for chatting or as a net: a free verse affair, whose slant
posts mark random stresses in my hammering head
from a day of struggle with storms, refusing to say *I can't.*

Good poets make bad fences? It would be consolation.
Where's a critic when you want one to lob back a comment
on our old glass shower door or this new exhibition

of headboards from our first double bed, exposed
to neighbourhood watch, or me unable to do the job,
too proud to call in a man? Would I have been roused

to this pitch of frustration had I not conveniently forgotten
that when we first moved in there were no fences at all,
a right of way ran clear across four gardens?

What now we call the back was then the front: a well,
a copper, coal-house, privy; and tales of the night soil
collector who would trot across and beyond this very pale

I'm lying beside and trying to fix, but failing. *Shit!*
*Shit!* The answer, Frost, undoubtedly is: bad fences
make bad tempers. Calm it. Consult the Net.

*

A circuit in the half light on New Year's Eve,
repeating to Rosie the word 'gloaming', while her sister awaits
reels and gales on Prince's Street. In our lane, the river

has swelled the old ford's tune to a pibroch of hyperbole
the bridge would rather not hear, plucking at its piers,
strumming poplars, trying to garotte the field maple.

The floodgates to the citysomething houses are lying open
like giant on-off switches. The windows are all dark
as if there is nothing to power. The old year's grey hopes

are erased in a reel-to-reel fast-forward mix
of clay, sewage, fertilizer. One time we would have
played a game on the bridge; tonight it is the Styx

and we only talk of bodies, much to our daughter's
disgust, who snatches the pink Christmas wind-up torch
and beams us clear (with our thank-you notes) of the dark waters.

*

The mother at the end of Hatchet Lane howls for her calf.
The field at the back of our house – all spiky set-aside – drains
away the incessant January rains. There is sunshine enough

to make these walkers believe it's spring. The squirrels are already
converts and they hurry to worship. Over the barbed wire
where sludge from the lake was spread, there's movement. Sunday

is creeping to life and I am holding a carbon festival of wreath
and bough, shrub sacrifice, fence and trellis offerings.
Fire blazes and I hose it down. As I prod, from beneath

the griddled sticks – a hedgehog, writhing, horribly scorched.
What should I do? Try drowning it in the pond? No use,
it swims, so I hook it on the fork, dump it under the hedge

and wait for the fire to burn down. My conscience hibernates,
while – out of the embers – nails, staples, screws raise their
accusing prickles at me. The creature vanishes overnight.

*

There is always waiting: on the phone, online, or in a layby
at a bus-stop that has no timetable, knowing the bus
has either gone or doesn't exist. Or with a crying baby

in the doctor's, name after name called, and the interfering
smile of one who talks and another you might have taught
who's waited all these years to tell you … Or you're standing in pouring

Monday outside the butcher's to Friday at the post office
or the bank or waiting for coal. Something will turn up. The golden
hosts (*please take your cash*) are pushing through clay and there are cafés

on the pavement again and we are ready to be served, to taste
a coffee that hasn't cooled, to get the bill, to pay
and let the lights change: home for an appointment and a fasting

blood test. The butcher is empty now. They are closing
the post office. We sit and wait for the news at 6
and 7 and 10. To hear how badly England are losing.

For the weather. And a trail for something on Egypt. Finish writing
your diary, lock up desire, let sleep make you drop *The God
Delusion* and enter your dream – the one where you are always waiting.

*

In Keyston, the hacked clay waits for a memory stick.
Daffodils hunch like PC objectors to Good Friday's
mowing ritual. I have tried the church door. It's locked

and Alpha Dot Security have left the world their hologram.
I'd hoped to find some memorial to the lover and divine
who held the living here, inside – instead, as I am

texting you and Huntingdonshire's dead give stony
silent rebuff to the A14, reversing lorries,
jets, and one lone collared dove – it's Donne

himself who climbs, ignoring me, not quite believing
he's agreed to this outlandish benefice (the roads
knee-deep from London) to please his wife. A *living*?

His roving years are past and yet that country moll
who wouldn't catch his eye is enough to make him wish
the gargoyles would stop poking tongues; and to recall

another girl, then others, row on row, their features,
lips and breasts, but not their names. The busy lover
would have carved them into these divine grey beeches.

The tower's shadow ticks. He must have felt the arch
conceal its burden as he touched this warm stone, breathing
stained light, then slipped out through the porch.

A bell tolls and down goes that unruly sun.
His wife's expecting their next child; but by next year
*John Donne. Ann Donne. Un-done.*

Four centuries. For us, it's thirty years; and still
you share a poet's bed and send me words from 'The Ecstasie'.
Keep texting love: that brief vibrating thrill.

\*

Soon, the karts will have started up and scared off the lark
idling invisibly over Rookery Farm. On the airfield road,
May blossoming into rape and high cirrus, I snake

around nothing, though there were hedges once, elms, and huts
where girls sprawled out of nose cones into prairie dreams.
From converted station to chapel to where the A-road cuts

Spaldwick from all the Giddings with its psalm to residual
nesting ground, meadow, set-aside, I freewheel home.
Twenty-five years ago I walked through the middle

of a summer night to reach you. At this Z-bend, I still
remember finding the sign I had been looking for, where today
there is a fox, tame, in someone's garden, with collar and bell.

*

Blossom that falls almost as soon as it's shrouded the bones
of our apple trees – the three of them, two from the long
banished auctioneer, Warner's King, and one Orleans

Reinette, rough, acidic still, never the sweet
regime the Brigadier promised. Since it's Bank Holiday,
we thought we'd drive to the Orchard Tea Garden, meet

Brooke, Woolf, Russell, Forster – but so many cars
and it's raining, we might not even make it out of our books.
Home, then. Free verse. Let others crowd at the bars

to Jeffrey Archer's house. Tiny apples have appeared
as the boughs round off their pole dance. May, and my pencil
is plaiting music to which only she knows the words.

*

*for Rosie*

Walking to your old school, the way we used to, down Carnaby
and past the magic garden with that tiny artist's studio
you so envied, locked and decaying now, towards a colony

whose taste demands bread, who receive instead our duck
impressions, over the Kym (brimming with stories of how
it rose and flooded, of manhole geysers, canoes in the park)

up to the cemetery gates. Through and beneath the Cedar's
branches, propped so they will not crush our local names,
Eaton, Stratford, Coles, with the force of Lebanon, to where

Toad Hall poop-poops and we're at Overhills. What's changed?
The playground. A pink house and a green. You indulge your memories
and here, perhaps, is where our walk should end – with those caged

exotics singing from someone's garden a community song
of jungle pleasure, scribbled trees, a crayoned smile
and each day blu-tacked to the sky. But we have swung

away from the doctor's surgery, down Ashfield and over
the narrow bridge below the darkling youth club,
where mist has already begun to sign itself in as river.

# PASTORALS

(1990–1998)

*I behold*
*The tumult, and am still.*

Cowper

## EPITHALAMION
*for Stephen and Elizabeth at St James's, Piccadilly*

St James peers down his tunnel vault again
at one more couple waiting to pass through:
three hundred years of wedding days since Wren
bestowed on him this virgin site. Now you
have chosen, as the year's late hybrids bloom,
to swell to bride and groom
where William Blake was dipped in Gibbons' font
and wept all innocence; and where through gloom,
his pack of sins at bay on one last hunt,
they lay old Queensberry; and where explorer
Sir Samuel Baker swore
his wife would share all goodly worlds, possess
all lakes, all rapids, cataclysmic falls
and know their very source ... But now God calls
St James to do his work and promptly bless
the happy pair, unless
they leave without his touch, his scallop seal
and all the bells of London let their blessings peal.

St James descends before young Eros flies
or wedding ghosts can rise with songs to fledge.
But here's one, glory bulging in his eyes
and inkstains on his voice: *True marriage!*
sings Blake. *For here both love and pity meet.*
*By you, each chartered street*
*is lit and hung with signs of* Peace on Earth.
*In your soft care, the hopes of London beat,*
*though powerless to change the stars of birth ...*
He sighs and points where underneath the pew
beside him is Old Q
on all fours – raked out ashes of a dray
condemned to harrow dark and frigid vaults –
*This hour brings light and loosening of bolts.*
*This warmth melts cold dismissal into May,*
*your sunrise splits our grey,*
*the wounds my age knew may your new age heal*
*and all the bells of London let their blessings peal.*

St James is stretching out – but two last shades
come weaving up the aisle a tack of troth
between the slave and drug and ivory trades
across a swamp of purple-flowering growth
the size of England. Fresh-baked from the Nile,
surviving on its wild
water life and honey dreams of a source,
*You may get trapped!* Sam Baker calls, *enisled!*
*And if you do,* adds Florence, *there's no force*
*will shift you once you've made yourselves a slave*
*to how the winds behave.*
*So move, move on, on* – And as they fade,
the Saint has blessed you both, Elizabeth, Steve:
the church's past swings open to receive
your future here where all its tracks are laid
and ready to be played:
our hearts turn bell-metal, bob the joy we feel –
and all the bells of London let their blessings peal.


## FIVE WALKS WITH OUR BEST MAN
*(1992–1997)*

Our first walk, there was a return to power.
Across the blue South Downs, sunning themselves,
those two staunch windmills, Jack and Jill, were not
for turning. But you looked swept off your feet.

Our second walk, we talked the middle stretch
of the Thames, remembering those girls upriver
we'd desired, and skirting the high fancy walls
of Hampton Court, or Kew – my push-chair Eden.

Our third walk, there was such a scrim the one view
Glyndebourne afforded us was restricted.
We beat a line of plainsong, crossing the Ouse
where Miss Stephen drowned her moon-howling voices.

Our fourth walk, you drove us out of dawn's green belt
to Leith Hill, past Meredith's grove of yew,
past views like back projection to our song-and-dance
of Jung and lost youth and the growing children.

Our fifth walk, returning to the New Forest,
where, at seventeen, we chased down our own legends
to the Rufus Stone. Stag-heads in shadow now.
Wild ponies; a young buck; the sound of rutting.


## AT THE ELEVENTH HOUR
*for Daniel, born 11th November 1993*

Born into remembrance. While we observed
two minutes' silence, you made the Great Push
from no-man's-land. While pensioners, unnerved
three-quarters of a century, stood crushed,
you cried in triumph. While some who had served
were named as breathing mist in the brief hush,
you made your landing on a spit of peace
thrown up by war, and said that pain should cease.

You are for the next hundred years, not ours.
And though we all go over the top at once,
there will be those who ask: where are the flowers
that used to vein the fields from here to France?
And those who plough on, senseless as the powers
instructing them, and make their blind advance
in one huge combine harvester, where youth
is reaped and at the same time threshed from truth.

Of all their silos yield, of all their mill
grinds to flour, remember this crumb: that we,
whom Alzheimer's or a shot of morphine will
have wiped clean of our unstaunched century,
we puffed at its dandelion clock until
we dreamt a flower our children's time might see.
So, little rootball of your parents' genes,
take stock, and shoot, and show what Daniel means.

## Moving

Rooks like dust in a home
movie spatter the view
through the picture window
as we peck at belongings
in your grandmother's bungalow,
vacated now, up for sale.
*The Natural History of Selborne,*
an Egyptian tea towel,
rusting weights and scales ...
What can we do with this
cracked windmill? that springless
cuckoo clock? Now that she's
bent into the storm-force
of her ninety-fifth year,
does she need this Shakespeare?

A gull outside peels like
a dressing where the barbed wire
was surgically removed
and the poppies trampled
by the intruders who came
deep in a summer's night.
Below that slope they parked
invisibly and loaded into their van
things that you do not see today.
There is no escape mechanism
ticking in the hall now.
No willow-pattern blue
to glaze the emptied rooms.
Only detritus, only utility.
Only the rooks calling for more.

## GOG AND MAGOG

Chalk giants, brothers in a sumo match,
we wrestle nightly, not moving, but always
ready to move, seeking that point of stillness,
that universal posture, from which all
action springs. When you were young, your parents
walked you here, across the downs to Wilmington:
no eyes, no movement or strength, two uprights
providing symmetry, keeping order,
my sexlessness preventing embarrassment.
Then, when you were married, you stopped the car
at Cerne Abbas and photographed the stark
manhood of my opposite, the restless
muscles of Hercules, his knobbly club
rampant across the country. Now to the low
hills of Gogmagog you bring your children
where there is little to be seen of us.
But if they ask you, tell them Beowulf,
St Paul, Boötes, Thor; tell them surveyor,
haymaker, warrior … History teacher,
tell them the time we tell is of the stars,
and show them in their own earth's chalk their smallness.

## ROADS

Convenient, no doubt: a short-cut across
the site of Naseby Field, making at last
the M1 accessible. The past is past:
a haywain rutted deep; a dead shire horse
blocking the way; the choice between your purse
or your life. So, never mind the open-cast
incision in our gut, or that the fast
lane overtakes these grey crawlers who cross
at night on ineradicable routes –

controlled explosions – rusted spiky mines –
or that these moon shapes drop out of the air
to mate with kindred eyes of one who hoots
welcome, then obliterates the white lines.
Never mind, so long as we're getting there.

*

Red Route, Green Route – the touting and debate
run on as endlessly as the traffic will,
as if at a ball-bearing's whim: a still,
unhurried valley, where a couple, of late,
have loved to walk, two pensioners who hate
roads, who don't drive, knowing merely the skill
of catching bus or train, or from this hill
seeing the crucible in which words create
solutions, and thinking where will it end?
With by-pass operations, till the heart
gives out? The head spins. Will Government spend
our birthright on this lavish new roulette
of tolls and roundabouts? Another bend,
and there's a closed pit, a car that won't start.

*

A stretch of open moorland. Park the car,
and climb past sheep and ponies up a track
that should (the map says) take us where one black
dotted line meets one red. Have we come too far?
Perhaps there's nothing left to see of *Sarn
Helen*, the road named for a woman dragged
to Rome by the Governor of this last tract
of empire … The children wonder why we are
out here instead of on the golden train
to Eurodisney. The Romans are revered
for this, their legacy (we try to explain):
an unsurpassed, uniquely engineered
network of … facts that are greeted stony-eared,
like Trojans greeting Paris, home again.

*

The first time we have let her on the road.
Her independence paid for with our fear,
as one small gold-and-silver frame goes veering
on to the verge to let a serpent-load
of scaly greens, a slurry-guzzling toad,
baleful giant, or dragon in red gear
that licks our hedges, pass. She's learnt to steer,
thank God, and signal too, the way I showed
last time we rode out. Nothing pleased her more
than my pronouncing her road-worthy, grown up
to join the brotherhood of spokeless wheels.
It's hard now to remember how it feels,
that first free-plunging run down from the top,
here on the far side of all she's waiting for.


## Pass

The mist lifted enough for us to enter
Hardknott Pass. The notice beyond the sheep
warned it was not to be tried in winter:
single track, hairpin bended, and as steep

as one in three. Into our sight come clear
blue visions, then cataracts, and grey clouds
stoop towards the rocks. But safe in low gear,
my parents seemed happier – there were crowds

doing the same, after all. Wind down the glass
and span with a haiku that narrow space
between styles. All images in this pass
translate to our secure iambic pace.

And only when unchildlocked for the cairn's
plunging view down to the walls of Hardknott Fort,
where legionaries patrolled a high square
nailed shut against all exultant thought,

did we glimpse a map laid out – and my mother
a girlhood path that she and best friend Pearl …
lost since the war, now somewhere in another
world, South Africa, she thinks … The road's curl

a black ribbon untwining from a love
journal. My mother clammed up. My father
provoking her to *climb down the rest of*
*the pass on your own now then, if you'd rather.*

## Building the Boat

From holt and weald they drag
extinct pines to be our keel,
while someone chips a flint.

From the New Forest they roll
oaks to be carved to inflected
Norman ribs, while someone

is melting copper with tin.
The Greeks give us olive pegs.
The Roman inspectorate moves in

to mark our water-line. And all
is caulked with the bees-wax
from a dissolved distant priory.

On the prow is a plaque of laurel
with our dates and a painted eye
in green acrylic. Safely below

and rigged in Egyptian white linen,
a Californian Big Tree someone
has forged a way of holding in irons.

But our oars are of Norse ash: heave now
towards the Black Sea whose huge waves
rear, long over and not yet.

## THREE ANGLO-SAXON POEMS

*BEOWULF*

England is a dark hall:
all the warriors
have gone to their pallets.

And Grendel is dead.
We can sleep soundly, though
Mildenhall is unclosed –

its sparrow will rip through
and out the far door
before the red glow fades.

But Grendel is dead.
We can dream of peace
and restructuring and open

house. Unless … From across
the dream, out of the peat,
unwithered, familiar, sexy

as a Black Madonna, she comes:
the armed, avenging anima
born of our foetal posture.

## THE LONGSHIPS

Believe what we could not. That there –
like mussels on a bare rock, massed
and open for our swords to slice
the byssus – were Christ's fishermen
in cells of silk and gold.

On a cold easterly we skimmed
last spring: now, feather in riches
here until the autumn, when gales
from the west will heave this light
out of Lindisfarne, Jarrow, Whitby.

The inhabitants of these dream shells
would not fight, never fly, but gazed
(as if books had always been clouds)
like puffins on a ledge construing
mist, elucidating the breakers.

### SUTTON HOO

Not the marinated
head of Lindow Man,
but the old darkness
takes this helm.

Silver clings to it:
creatures out of their
element, bronze worm-
cast from the grave.

When the sleepy armies
of dragon-slayers
approach the hoard
with pencils, with clipboards,

the sword and shield
of advancing education,
though they wake, they see
nothing for the gleam.

Pupils dilate
fantastically, as
they stare into their
own dark age.


## BIRCH

Canoe or witch's
broom at the bottom

of the garden: escape
from the day of fire

or the day the scalp-
chilling ice-caps

grind their war-path
and our only comfort

against the red clay
in which we bury

frozen hoards
of gold and silver

is gold and silver
of the forest malls

where we will live on
postcards, bootsoles,

pennybuns and
bark-bread, bark-bread.

## BELL CORNER
(from *Crossing the Heath*)

A bell hangs where the roads divide
that never peals
but from the left-hand fork flow weird
ungainly reels.

And there a woman stands alone
and strokes gut strings
begging with pluck and constant drone
ungodly things.

The silent right-hand road is mine
whose only jigs
are gibbets where the highwaymen
unbow their legs.

## NIGHTFLIGHTS

Then (the Mauls say) the only airport here
was Heston, where Mr Chamberlain took off
for Munich. They had heard the peaceful cough
of his pistons from their greenhouse, whose bleared
panes crack with Boeings now so I can't hear
their words about the war, but see the rough
remains of their shelter and the stone cover
to their well, and wish … But my parents' fear
permits me only to dream of those unseen
dark places. Nightflights wink into the west
across our hawthorn hedge, towards a Heath
silence has stamped out like something obscene.
I go to bed, and with a tightening chest
lie there, wait, listen, and invent a myth.

## UNDER THE FLIGHT PATH

My entrance is a cul-de-sac off Hounslow Heath,
once feared for masked hold-ups, an airport now,
characterless; but in that ambrosial flask

are sealed these precious vagrants on a patch
of mid-century. Britannias above them
feathering home, Tridents puncturing

extended conversation like a banjo skin –
and in the memory, the head's resonating
membrane, string still answers string ...

Here, 'King Menzies' rolls out of his sleek taxi,
home to his mint Arabia collection,
his opera boxed sets; and his Persian wife,

who loves her cockatoo, takes in stray cats,
and will leave him for a mongrel, knocks
and keeps knocking at our door for sugar;

while, through our party wall, 'The Peasants',
hammer and tongues, young newly-weds (who outside
speak softly of fishing and babies) spit fire;

as 'Boudicca', next door but one, crashes back
in her Anglia, ticket equipment slung at her breast,
from battle on the Bath Road's bloody buses.

Or as, along my secret cinder-and-ash backway,
the Crops' son carries his cleft palate,
deaf smile, and a box (for me) full of Superman;

past Old Man Withinshaw, who'd shout as I picked
pale and skeletal lanterns near his chicken run,
whose granddaughter looks out from her leukaemia,

*Going to see Lord Jesus* ... Next door, the teacher's
daughter knows Paul McCartney; next door, the surgeon
is flying Tim and Toot to South Africa; next door,

the Major's son has been given permission to ride
a motor scooter, and shows me his home-made rifle,
and cowboys every midnight below my window,

plucking love on the banjo's neck. There's Elaine,
my pal from primary school, all at once
blonde, leggy and my pal no more. And there's

Sally, limping down the ash-and-cinder alley,
one leg too long, leaning into her viola case
and lisping to the Great West Road. Other,

mysterious, neighbours also: the brothers
on the corner, their high-walled garden,
shy nocturnals. And gay birds like the Kellys,

ever flitting off to Heathrow pyjama parties,
free passes to the world's airspace. And once,
they flew me in their Morris Minor to Littlehampton.

Does Concorde still shiver my bedroom? Is Eve there
trilling a war song on her lawn to intercept it
above our air-raid shelter? Next-door-but-

twenty-odd-years, who are those furred and haughty,
horn-rimmed and raincoated, unspeaking caricatures?
The Brittens: they keep chained a cartoon bulldog

and are pure Aryan. But it's old Mr Mortimer
and old Mr Wheeler, double-digging the trenched
alluvium of their days, who speak the silence

gone with orchard, heath and pond; and one of them
was visited one day by a crew-cut American boy
I wanted to impress with my Gemini bike act:

seeing the door is closed, instead I hurry home
with my prize astronomy project, like a genie
aborting take-off, dropping back into the bottle.

*Clinton, New Jersey*

## ON CHIEF TAMENUND'S MOUNTAIN
*for Mike Petrus*

An empty Bud Light
dropped where the leaves
are dropping these last
days of September.

Taking it by the scruff
of its plastic cross,
you curse the bastard
who let it fall –

but then catch the feel
of another, wilder shape
in your hand: one stone
picked from others

identical, only this
hurled into the heart
of a black bear or used
to tear at its hide.

You trail the throwaway
down to where the cars
and the trash-cans are,
but keep in your bag

(trees lumbering into
blackness, towards bareness)
that permanently sealed
vision of a lost way.

*Delaware Water Gap*

## BOB'S WORD

Three raccoons were shot in the road
outside our house this week – rabid,
says Bob – been out attacking cars.

A woman who shot two cops escaped
from the open prison here, Bob says:
a car drew up and she just got in and went.

Bob was divorced once, but soon
remarried the same woman, and now
his lawyer won't speak to him.

New York is lawless and home
to so many homeless, he tells us,
they hibernate all winter in the store fronts.

Bob describes how his boss's eyes
self-seal in the envelope
print-shop where he works. Lyme Disease.

If you don't have health insurance,
Bob says, you're dead. They clean
you out, take everything.

Raccoons are the cleanest creatures,
says Bob – they wash themselves
with hands like humans.

## TIGHTROPE

Diving is nothing. But paying out a hawser,
cable-laid, three inches in diameter,
thirteen hundred dollars long, to span Niagara,
Blondin the Great has come.

Paying is nothing. But to stretch manila fibres
taut, from America's Pleasure Grounds to Canada,
fasten them with eighteen guy-ropes, admit the world for
twenty-five cents each.

To boast is nothing. But to step on to that cable,
walk halfway and drop a bottle on a string to
crowds below, then up and drink the contents,
cheers, and off again.

To walk is nothing, but to run along the tightrope,
somersault, in darkness, on stilts, or do it backwards,
blindfold, in irons, on a bicycle, or once even
pushing a wheelbarrow.

To impress is nothing, but to leave the watchers speechless,
carrying a stove out to the centre, cracking eggs and
cooking a perfect omelettte, eating it, then lowering
portions to pleasure boats.

To be famous is nothing, but to be preserved on camera
carrying one's manager across, and recorded offering
piggybacks to a Prince, His Royal Highness whispering:
*Thank God that's over!*

To be a stuntman. Nothing. But – to be Blondin.
Retire to an English estate and title it 'Niagara',
die in your bed at the far end of a full span:
the greatest of all stunts.

## NIAGARA

Don't think about after you've crossed the Falls:
Niagara Gorge, the rapids, where above
a man is walking tightrope with a stove
strapped to his back, and ahead there are calls
from a honeymoon couple caught when the walls
of their ice bridge collapsed. Just try to prove
the glory of this place is like true love,
indestructible ... I'm over. My barrel's
about to smash down in Canada. When I'm
a shape (unnoticed by those blue-robed hordes
boarding their ferry to cross the wild Styx)
pinned under plunge and sensation and time,
tell that girl, the rainbow girl throwing me words
inflatable, kiss shaped, I'm done with tricks.

## ICE HOCKEY IN TIME OF WAR
*a Midwinter Night's Game*

Padded to look like men,
faceless, behind iron grilles,
and wielding sticks huge
as tactical battle equipment,
these dumb mechanicals swerve
across the ice and collide
with cheers from parents, packed
in front of hazy screens.

Every now and then a siren
goes off and the young
leave the arena like body-bags
while reinforcements are lured
on to the ice by a puck
that will reduce them all to asses.

## KATIE IN A PROSPECT OF D.C.

Outside the Oval Office
my daughter started
to sing Humpty Dumpty.

Then, at a rising black wall
that dropped to a V,
she stopped singing and cried

for a flag of stars
to wave past the dark
windows of the Space Museum.

On Capitol Hill, she
chattered towards a life-
size image of Jesus,

was silent before the statue
of the Father of Television,
heard the floor whisper.

But approaching Watergate,
she pressed her investigative nose
to the glass, and broke in

on our conversations again
and again to report
what all the king's men couldn't.

## SELF-PORTRAIT ON INDEPENDENCE DAY

The day starts with me becoming a horse
for my daughter, then – with a jolt – the king
to whom she brings gifts: a pillow, a belt,
a shoelace (I ♥ HOMER on it), a coaster
of a cardinal bird, mobile from string
and 'snake fur'. She styles herself The Great Melt –

Merlin, is she thinking of? – until the air's
abuzz with katydids saying 'There's a sword
needs pulling from this day if you're to succeed
to its imaginary throne.' Cars speed
in search of the parade; our groundhog scares
home to its woodpile. My quest is for a hoard

concealed behind the White Dragon. Tonight,
America will breathe her fire to mark
the day they were ex-Englished. She's not afraid
of one small insect dynamo in the dark
bookshelves as her explosives start to light
the sky beyond the Liberty Parade,

but he, is he – who chose to take her back
centuries later, and watched the coarse jokes
crackle, patriotism go pop, candour
snuffed out, but said nothing, browsing near oaks
and wondering only, as Desert Thunder
electrified the world, what else might crack –

is he afraid and does he feel and could
anyone say that they had heard him talk
with passion of anything? Perhaps the times
when tameness roared and drove him to the woods
with Iron John (But who … ?) for a ritual walk
to the Black Bear (But where … ?). Missing the rhymes

of his native landscape, he made good friends
with free verse wilderness that, when it lay
frost-glazed, could blank the night's three thousand miles
in promises. Baneberry thickets, piles

of heartwood from Black Mountain, such dead ends
returned his feet to the more travelled way

to learn that what united states fear most
is solitude, mystery … These I have tracked
along faint Indian trails, followed traces
of musk-rat, mink and beaver, caught in the act
sometimes, off balance, rocks a-quiver, the ghost
of a goddess haunting lost dark places …

America, I do not love you: have found
too much of the old world surviving here –
a chat-show host, whose genial 'I am it'
voice-over informs us stars will appear
tonight through the support of … Follow shit,
and soon enough we'll come to common ground.


SATELLITE

A dish points outwards from our outside wall
to what we cannot see: stars that know all
more clearly than these nightly Movie Greats
the fate of earthen empires. The new estates
that blinker us from crystal ballroom spaces,
haul us on in their fibre-optic traces,
plough constellations; with a flash of shares
u-turning, leave the Great and Little Bears
extinct and gilt-edged bars of progress furrowed
down the land's face. All that we have is borrowed:
museums full of stuffed trophies slowly
decaying. Territories that tick. Holy
marbles seeming to breathe. Even these words I
mix to purity, and this island time
we live on, living off serials, then soap,
and lastly just news – that shooting green hope
our parents plotted as the world turned red,

not with sunset, nor shame, but foreign dead.
We wait, hungry, now we have cleaned the Great
from Britain, scraped it out, shrunk it, wait
for a force beyond this uttermost storey
of our high rise, a column whose glory
will be to have relieved us of our fame,
of all that mafficking, cheering of a name
picked blind from a skull and nailed to the sky.
The dish receives its message from on high
in beams that swaddle the earth, in curves
of parabolic reckoning, then serves
us word made flesh: chained bare Salome sprawled
before us, while Civilisation's bald
chronicler slots between those repeats of Wars
for King and Country networked in the stars.


## HOLST

Marching into prayers at primary school
they used to play a 78 of *Mars*.
There began my love of music
and of astronomy. The perfect fool
had found his round peg's round hole:
to sing squarely of the stars
to a generation who would lose its
sight and hearing before it had grown old.

## THE TRIUMPH OF TIME

Boulez leafs through the great score
and a score of leaves
falls like that season

ticket for the Proms
his parents granted their budding
genius, hoping he would blossom

and grow leafy with Brahms,
but as the autumn drew on
he was acquiring a taste

for the sour and dark fruit
of his age. *Listen to this
Birtwistle,* he would say

and whistle it, spitting out
the Stones, getting high on
Brueghel. The parade is

an arena full of young
idealists facing the roar
of empire. It passes

and here are the old,
the confused, like a mural
on a wall beside a staircase

to private inaccessible apartments.

## QUARTET FOR A ROW OF TERRACED COTTAGES

First violin begins the theme: plainsong
in apple white, a bloom of the sixties, neither
pretty nor bland, yet eastern flavoured, heat
in clay bricks. It hides a small, greenish spark
which keeps on growing, knowing always that once
there grew a sycamore above its sound-box.

Second mirrors the row: a centrifugal
force opens the shared manoeuvring
towards outer space. A touch of a jig
from Ireland, some Italianate trills
and ornamentation, the smiled acceptance
of any wild dissonance from the first.

Viola keeps at arm's length: the ambitious chug
of a fiddle outgrowing its natural size,
self-consciously dull, gawky, wants to be
a bass line, an oak-beamed original,
but cannot shake the restless mobile grind
of hurdy-gurdy tunes, that gay vulgarity.

Cello knows the long rest is coming, and draws
from its simple well the deepest, oldest tears.
Destined to be low, never to rise or move,
but enjoying others' fireworks, it inhabits
the four autumnal rooms of its clef, desires
no solo, dreaming of song, sweet cadences.

## LISTENING FOR NIGHTINGALES

All the birds of the dusk
sound beautiful. Is there one
that sounds true, that empties

a dark jug drunkenly
as Grafham Water raises its
$H_2O$? Ah, Keats

I envy you your certainty.
I too would fly by nightingale
if I could be sure that that

that's like a spring stuttering
out of a broken pipe were the pure
original song, and not

a drug on the market. Such black
burdens the wings of my enchantment,
it plunges off the green grid

and there is nothing. That magic
flew with your age,
and leaves me in the dark with mine.

## *from* THE TWILIGHT OF THE BIRDS

### *THE LODGE, SANDY*

The birds' Valhalla, where at dusk they will come
for the last time and chorus to the earth,
to the fields that are by now shaved clean

of hedgerow, seedpod, stubble, snail.
They will not trouble to debate the issues
passerines have discussed since Chaucer's day –

there is just one way to go: a pilgrimage
to the shores of extinction. The woodpecker
taps their doom in his hanging-cap

and the owl pronounces a verdict on whom-
soever it consumes. The birch leaves burn
out of the sand, and the only sound

is that dry crackle on the night air.


### *GAUDEAMUS IGITUR*

What was that we heard
trapped behind the firescreen
in the staff common room?
No singing, just a desperate
thrashing of wings, as if
the ghost of one of that flock
of black-gowned, beaked
sadistic masters had dropped
back to inspect his ingle,
beating the ignorant soot.
Was it the same stunned
bundle I found by my study
having collided with that ring
of invisible fire, my vitrified
desire not ever to teach?

*TRING*
*for Michael Walters*

At Tring, you guarded a treasury
of the world's eggs, and showed me
that hoard – more precious than Fabergé's
or Fafner's – each egg
a world seen from the apogee
of your craft, keeping its own
atmosphere and global features,
its fabulous lineage, which I
can't now recall, only drawers
like an instrument panel, and rows
of gridlocked shells, the life
blown out of them, their skin-deep
fascination, fragile as eyes.

When the skies above Hertfordshire
are merely home to the Boeing
and the common fighter bomber, these
will still soundlessly glide
open to lay before us
like a lost secret of air
traffic control, your wards:
their speckles, streaks and scrawls.

*NIGHT CALLS*

Our local doctor
tells of his horror
of owls

of how they will gaze
surgically into your
soft tissue

from the far side of
their barred habitat
their spell of solitary

or wing into your beams
on the way to a
head-on crash

they hoot like doom's
emergency service
and they stand

rubber-necking in the fog
when motorway
madness strikes

their shrieks are the new-
born dead
taking to the darkness

## ON THE GREAT NORTH ROAD

Above all, look up from your feet
as John Clare did, and notice
that raptor about to claim a mouse,
the map of small-holdings on that bark,
those regimented limes outside the manor
growing openly more heartless.

The sky today is unenclosed.
It changes like the English landscape.
Look up, and see with Clare's eye –
without the elaborate golden frame
of elm leaf Taste dictated
they should hang him in, their private

view of bird's-nest and mouldiwarp
Northamptonshire, its measured
rectangular plots. That's not
for you out on the road. Look up.

You have new lenses in your frames,
plastic, scratch-proof, glazed

within the hour by Vision Express
just off the road Clare limped down
invisible. Look up. A cardboard box.
The New Age and its litter
ageing in a layby. Asylum seekers
on the verge. A discharged patient

lost among rape fields. Our country
changes, has not changed. Who cares
in the community of crow and owl?
Above all, unlock, see the face
from the removal van, the figures
at the hospital reception, not simply

the Fenland sunset you're driven towards.


JOHN GURNEY AT BEDFORD MIDLAND STATION

Bedford Midland. A stooping Horus hawk
above the mind's abandoned aerodrome
checks at the barrier. *John?* Our shock
dumb-synchronised. *John!* I in monochrome,
pain-striped for a funeral, you travelling
light to grandparenthood. And suddenly, in
one surprise roll, we are unravelling
a rainbow, enter an inverted spin
through ether, phlogiston, prana, to where
Egypt opens its lotus chute. Aerial
displays that – like the station signs we tear
past blindly – soon prove immaterial,
as King's Cross/St Pancras brakes all dreams
but yours: you sit there, gliding to the Thames.

# GASCOIGNE'S EGG
## (1995)

*to the late John Gurney,*
*aviator, epic poet, and man about Bedfordshire*

Note:

*The poem contains references to strange events around the time of the maiden flight: these are recounted in John G.Fuller's* The Airmen Who Would Not Die.

## GASCOIGNE'S EGG

*Elizabethan poet, George Gascoigne, returns to*
*his birthplace, Cardington, site of the Royal*
*Airship Works, where the R101 was built.*

Returning from an empire-long redundancy
to construct this, I choose the most flexible
form, a doped skin, and bags

of inflammable stuff. My name decayed
into a pseudonym: The Green Knight, giant
who kept on coming (even headless) to Sir Gawain

each New Year. I am not here to play tricks
but to tell the story that begins where I began,
in Cardington. Pass the cup around

and let those drink who thought to raise
their names on a dream of empire-building –
an Avalon from which they might never wake.

\*

Oblivion is what most poets expect.
But not the Secretary of State for Air
who sees the future in two hangars:

in the first, the state-fed R101,
in the second, Vickers' own pet R100.
In both, the engineers find dark corners

to make love, above them the cloth and naked
steel-work of a nativity: it is here
the empire manufactures its name, the child

fathered by me and those who found
this world is not sufficient – who now know
why the lilies toil not neither do they spin.

Working in the next shed – prosaic truth –
is Nevil Shute, who visits and hears
the engineers whisper sweet nothings:

101's construction too rigid
101's useful lift too small
101's elegant dance-floor tilts ...

But poetry is never rational – and blind
to the antics of the heavier-than-air clowns
overhead, their tragi-comic appearances –

the History of Hinchliffe, the Heroic Rise
of Lindbergh, the Knights of the Burning Piston ...
Poets? Why, we run on laughing gas!

*

Gold-beater's skin, it is called, membrane
from the intestine of a cow: of this the bags
are made, ten-storey high, that will lift

like long-winded folios, the airship
to immortality – intoning across the country
Willington  Welwyn  Hyde Park  Deal

and out among salt fantasies, the mouths
of the Nile and Indus, to anchor upon masts
tall as those I climbed and fought from.

Rigging on the air that plays the golden
pavan of an empire: the transparent skins
of hydrogen swell with courtly pride.

I would have scoffed when I was alive
at any immortality but literature, that light
which never shall decay, but which fell away

after months in the dark of a Spanish cell,
and looking back, strange to have gone down
just as my fortunes were rising, preparing

'The Grief of Joy', an imitation – in the days
one was not expected to be original – of Petrarch,
a New Year's Gift, I thought, for Her Majesty.

It is October. Nearing Hallontide. Our English
Zeppelin is preparing to go up. I died.
The mourners carried out the inflated corpse.

\*

To find yourself invisible to others – you might think
that's little more than the usual – but not
to be able to influence, only see and turn

friends cold with your presence, to be witness
to the consequences of your insincerity, to have nothing
to hide behind but your death … to be trapped

under glass like a portrait of the poet hanging
in the haunted gallery of a derelict manor –
that is hell. The heaven is being here

at all – much as one was – though pressurised
to continue the work, even in this shockingly
unpredictable, patched-up and volatile verse.

Stresses. Four thousand patches. A dream
of court, a fairy palace. On the tables
places for fifty laid in silver.

Weight a problem always, the five
pulsing iambic giant diesels
start up in the royal workshop.

In a London tea-room, a spark
flashes and Eileen Garrett cries
*Put off the flight!* but at the elevator

all visitors must wear tennis shoes,
the construction crew stand cheering,
travellers are insulated from any kind of shock.

\*

The Walking Parties. The mass unemployed
drag through the huge sliding doors
of Room 101. At my funeral, I flew

above my mother who wept that we had quarrelled
over a few silly sheep. I saw too
the tragedy on the faces of the watchers. But I

had died peacefully, detached from the mooring
mast and drifted up on a galliard, capering
to music of the spheres – barely changed

in that alembic, but remembering the crossbow
from Lord Grey, and my poem in reply, explaining
everything I had ever shot at I had missed.

'The Steel Glass' – our literature's first
blank verse is a blank in the memory;
the first tale of modern life, a blank;

the first masque, sonnet sequence, satire –
all blank. Deleted. I am famous for all
that is unknown. *Ferenda Natura* ... fame is

not the second hangar at Cardington,
the quietly virtuous and unblemished Vickers,
never in service to the state, and nowhere

commemorated. Master Shute is read by thousands.
My little Robin keep close your coin.
My lullaby sleeps tight in the anthologies.

\*

The story of Empire and of English poetry
is of innumerable repair jobs. Free verse
become the spidery structure of the ship

and metaphor the lighter-than-air lift for it –
but in an age whose longing has outstripped grey
polluted skies, whose desire is to go

beyond the grimy spheres, the moon
and smeared galaxies, into pure black
where time ends, your craft must carry you

out of a round world, as ours
sailed us free of the flat. In her apartment
Eileen Garrett enters a trance.

Fuel oil dumped over fields I used to stock.
The farmer, wise man, sues and collects.
I spent too much of my courtier's life

in the courts. Too many illusions to keep
aloft, to keep from crashing, to impress
the gawping crowds distracted by the fancy

displays around one. Now the pressure is on
to reach for the jewel in the crown, to pay for
this extravagance, to prove the qualities of endurance

of the British Empire. The proto-spitfires
irritate like mosquitoes in Karachi's heat,
but Lord Thomson of Cardington requests.

\*

Complexity is the downfall of grand enterprises.
They have had to bisect the airship to make
space for further airbags. Foreigners

have done just that for English poetry
(a sparrow chirps), left only this image
of dwarfish figures standing with bicycles

beside the cross-struts of a tail-section
in a French field that is all bare sky ...
I smell the gas leak of buried riches.

Science evolves, but which of the thousands
staring up look – or think to look – further
than the sliver of cleverness in their own eye?

In 'Gascoigne's Voyage into Holland' I said
man buildeth castles in the welkin wide
in hope to dwell with wealth and ease

but he the Lord can bind or loose ...
or something along those lines. But certainly
the imagery was all of climbing only to fall

and shipwreck was my theme, the loss of hope
and faith, looming despair. I see
the manor house where I was born, grew up,

and loved returning to, is demolished now.
A moat with nothing to defend. But words
like lady's-purse, like devil's-guts.


*


The Elephant-god is in the shadows, cross-
legged, smiling, hovering. And Horus
sharpens his talons and his beak, to guard

the feather of truth when it touches the scales.
The Algonquin drum their rain-dance to Mount Royal.
And beyond a town like Alice the inhabitants

already perceive what is to become of this
silver mirage: its story thrums
the song-lines. The mooring towers

parch in their precision-made locations.
The wind prowls on. The sun still
appears not to move. But change is coming.

A ton of dust snarls from the monster.
Dust of my family, dust of my home.
The hedges that began our conquest of the wild

have played their endgame, been lifted away.
History batters emptiness in Shortstown.
The Great Ouse meandering as uncertainly

as when last I stood gazing at the clouds.
Fancy farewell. Fancy farewell.
Sprawling in your direction a country park,

a garden centre, cable TV …
*Quoniam etiam humiliatos, amoena delectant.*
No books, the books are dust to dust.

\*

October rages, cursing at my heirs,
disinheriting all descendants. The appointed flight
into Egypt must go on: the beast is dragged

from its cleft at dawn, the crowds part,
the limousines approach to offer sacrifice.
The cheese blender – unseen – selects

the twenty varieties auspicious for this day.
Heavy, costly Turkey carpets brood
on greeting the High Commissioner for Egypt's

feet when the sun next rises.
Horus' eyebeam glints. The Elephant-god
maintains inscrutable ivory stillness.

It is not knowledge of the mysteries beyond
that makes for immortality in this world.
Shakespeare knew no more than I,

a mere boy actor on the river bank.
Language he was too young to enjoy
carried me, fought for me, and posted as spectacular

a claim to fame ... but it is that absurd
name orbits the globe, our spy
satellite, prelate of all intercourse.

Ask not the reason, any more than why it's
props that make the plane lighter than air,
prose that keeps the ghosts out of Baker Street.

*

So much depends on Lord Thomson's diary,
so little on what the Spiritual Alliance are hearing
at their round table. The passenger list

is ready, everything weighed and packed –
His Majesty's Secretary of State for Air,
the Director of Civil Aviation, all species

of flying creatures, feathered and chevroned
for the great migration. Fifty-four
dignitaries, officers and crew who knew

they were sailing off the edge of the known world
to where the men have heads in place of hearts. The ship
is nodding regally. The barometer falls.

Forced gaiety. How I remember it. No poet
but had to rise with a smile in front of Her.
The gold teeth it took, that courtly game ...

like these now, formed up in Air Ministry
trim, dark blue, with R101
in gold insignia. The clouds leaden,

the dizzy tower. Tiny silhouettes
and seven hundred and seventy-seven feet
of hydrogen. Dan Jove's cigar. The stink

of power. The glow of the dining salon's
wine, women and wilfulness. A messenger
dashes up clutching – Here be Monsters! –

*

The Certificate of Airworthiness. Like a knighthood
for an artist. Or a plaque in Poets' Corner.
There is one to Sir nothing Gascoigne in my church

and near it the ensign of this British legend.
The telegraph peals. Sparks sputter
from the exhaust. Each engine in turn.

Now all five, the senses that keep
empire from its Kraken sleep. Release.
A lurch – a sudden Victoria Falls –

half the entire ballast – the nose
turns up, up – a message in a wine glass –
STORMS RISING NOTHING BUT A MIRACLE
                                    CAN SAVE THEM

Encounters with a ghost ship in Hyde Park,
witnesses who speak to the cameras of a scraping
at their chimney pots, the red and green lights

spooking a mushroom field, the lovers fumbling
for last minute protection ... Behind celluloid,
champagne, cigars, intelligent conversation

about anything but the folly of all this –
leave that to those plimsolled labourers
prowling the catwalks, while the oil pressure

drops, the gas pressure drops, and the first
engine of the five predictably stops
over Hastings, into the dark night of *la Manche.*

*

Like reputation, this trip. Centuries it lasts
to the men who must drink, flirt, joke,
to the women waiting, to the children who will say

what they should not, and to the crewmen below,
caged, brooding on power eggs, listening
to the fifty-mile-per-hour winds, watching

each design fail, their parachutes humped
in sweat as the Black Bottom plays
and the whitecaps gleam. Pitch and roll,

yaw and dip, a sleepy progress
through a storm, held up by gold-beater's
skin – the cow jumps over the moon.

At Beauvais there is an hallucination in the sky
that circles like a dog looking for somewhere
to lie down, that leans against the cathedral

howling demon laughter, the heavens
staling down on garden, orchard, field,
the gale relentless. The ghost hound

sidles towards the woods. There is a poacher
setting traps here. Is it I? Gascoigne
of Cardington, the master of the beast that now

turns on him, wounded ... No. This demi-wolf
has no place in my 'Noble Art of Venerie' –
O Grey! if only I could just once hit the mark.

*

It falls, it drops. Digestion continues.
O grievous is the glee which ends in blood!
I stand accused within the court of taking

flesh not of my own ... but not the flesh
and blood of these who had survived France
twelve years before – to meet this holocaust

now the *nuée* comes, the poacher's wood
is in a blitz one hell-fanged man-trap
and all vainglory framed for the world

to publish – briefly, as if day had risen into
the darkness of man's mind. But no.
It was the blackout dawning. *Ever or never.*

*

Two colossi on the floodplain of the Ouse.
Huge and hollow. Time beats them
with its soft persistent fist till they roll out

R100, R101 in a tam-tam swell.
Dust whips and twists about them
like an Indian dancer, and the silent hubris

rises in imagination. Chrysalis of a myth
that flew into the flame, its power eggs
laid somewhere in Europe before it died,

Gascoigne's egg that became the silkworm
that shed and shed, until here: the Works
in Two Volumes. Save them from the fire.

*

# EUROPEAN UNION
## (1997)

*O Freunde, nicht diese Töne*

## EUROPEAN UNION

A wall is breached, the water levels rise,
subconsciousness begins to flood across
the bulb fields into the glass laboratories
that brought the sun to flower where bedrock was.
It flushes out secrets, unchequers yards
darkening in picture frames, sweeps them clear
of fruit and pheasant, old men playing cards
and all still life. It discovers a fear
of dry land, releases the swelling sail
of arrogant white power. It invades
the crow's-nest attic where a Jewish girl
is still in hiding. Its blitzkrieg persuades
Rotterdam to remember history,
old pasturelands abandoned to the sea.


2                                                      BELGIUM

Old pasturelands abandoned to the sea-
grey forest, whose hush-hush has drowned the cries
from those enmeshed in the mythologies
of war, since Flanders first meant territory
laced with needlepoint wire, knee-deep in dark
chocolate shell-holes, where the private dies
for general psychopathologies
to lie beneath an administrative block.
Before Waterloo, Napoleon was engrossed
in paperwork – a strategy recalled
by modern eurocrats: no clause too petty
to advance, no cause too vital to halt,
whatever the cries, the hush, the exhausted
slow hissing submission of industry.

3                                          *SWEDEN*

Slow hissing submission of industry
to the power that white water generates
like poetry that has its source in light's
black heart. In the high neutral territory
sacred to St Lucia, the committee
of Nobel, deep in its word-bunker, waits
to read the world the news: down endless nights
they slalom-skim a glaze of fantasy.
The paradox of darkness out of sun.
The irony of peace from dynamite.
The sheer chuckle of a literary prize
in Swedish, broached and bottled. One by one,
they gutter out – strange names – the same way that
tsunamis conquer and then colonise.


4                                          *DENMARK*

Tsunamis conquer and then colonise
the dragon-ship burial, the sacred ash,
the bog offering, the ribboned runic maze …
A sea-faring nation, harbouring a cache
of ancient currency, fears its plunder,
prepares to enact again the mighty clash
of Thor and Utgard Loki (the underhand
behaviour of the Frost Giant King
was paid for – as all Europe knows – in thunder):
the old woman Thor took on at wrestling
was really the World Serpent, the rich horn
he was challenged to drain had one end resting
in the sea … They say a wise warrior nurtures
the peace, burying storm-force under beaches.

5                                    GERMANY

The peace. Burying storm-force under beaches,
they move through the Christmas market stalls
*Unter den Linden*, paging their futures,
responding to commandments posters call
from a neatly mortared arcade wall
that thou shalt go on holiday next summer
to Dalmatia ... Slav workers in the mall
would surely say you should not have to fear
that someone near you might select this year
the carpets you laid last. It's time to change
your spots to different spots. Remember, here
you've always lived in petty princedoms – dangerous
to law-breakers, though down in Bonn
whatever crowns were once displayed have gone.


6                                     FRANCE

Whatever crowns were once displayed have gone,
but still they prize hard heads above these hearts
we like to think they're soft on – and those parts
for loving which were sickled, tied like corn
dollies, hung up, flung down, kicked, picked and worn
by heart-roasters, blood-toasters, tossed on a Cart-
esian errand through the uterine art
of romanticism, towards the throne
of modern Europe, carved from common bone
inlaid with pensées on necessity and chance,
studded with vital organs of advance ...
Card-holding revolutionary donors
to all who simply want now to quit France
on an air tour, their only jewel the sun.

7                                              *PORTUGAL*

On an air-tour, their only jewel the sun,
the well-oiled workers of the clockwork lands
head for a rainless world, unclouded fun
in neutral freedom, on natural white sands
from where the sea is just a video
of mindless rock and roll throughout the season:
no smoke, no sail, no subliminal man-o-
war tradition or imperial lesson
flash-framed. Only flies inspect the leftovers:
the earthquake site, the battle-ground, the sewage
hot-spots so seductive to their ancestors,
prepared for an enjoyable week's carnage
(though finding little turned yet on the beaches
to carrion), *affaires de coeur* with butchers.


8                                                *SPAIN*

To carry on *affaires de coeur* with butchers
approach the bull-ring called Democracy
passing polite refusal of white churches
towards the cervix of their ecstasy
passing the time-warped star-gaze of old watchers
towards the worm-hole in their galaxy
is knowledge how a people learn to grieve
is knowledge how a nation may survive
the transformation of an old boys' war
to what each Spanish man and woman craves
communion in a holy mass of gore
and flies and dust, to arise in waves
and cheer more hungrily the matador
circling a calm denial of mass graves

9 *GREECE*

Circling a calm denial of mass graves,
the generals dream of their Thermopylae,
the poets of a new myth-history,
the millionaires go dancing on the waves,
the tragic actors chant their speech and die,
the slaves have numbers for the lottery.
It has to be, this effort to restore
what otherwise our very fumes would eat,
these loving touches to young Nike's feet
ás if she tried on trainers. But in the roar
of Athens, as at Delphi, there is more
to find than when the old is made to meet
the new in a botched join. Strangers you greet
ask what that pride they boasted of was for.

10 *ITALY*

Ask what that pride they boasted of was for
as they attempt to keep the traffic running free,
the fountains playing, the tourist industry
awake – that creature closing in its paw
the wealth of those its rampant hunger tore
to pieces – tesserae of art history,
the Pantheon, Giotto, da Vinci:
it eats the Last Supper and it prowls for more.
Perhaps it was for Petrarch to have climbed
his mountain and slow-panned the crimes that love
had been and would be forced into by fame
and, having seen, to have sat down and rhymed
Laura with a truth that would never move:
these few cold peaks, a lyric verse, a name.

11                                              *AUSTRIA*

These few cold peaks, a lyric verse, a name,
and *Eine Kleine* in the coffee shop.
Vienna boys grow ears of purest grain,
whose music is the one unfattening crop
in this petite state. Slender resources
were forced to folds and whirls and creamy heights
by pressures from within, until psychosis.
And now, from a green couch, the mountain shouts
out Bruckner, the lake ringing Strauss Strauss Strauss,
as Schubert's hidden mill-stream fights the freeze
and Mozart avalanches the opera house,
Haydn goes on trimming Christmas trees
like Joseph when the angel first arrives ...
All dream of warmth, youth, kicking through dry leaves.

12                                              *LUXEMBOURG*

All dream of warmth. Youth, kicking through dry leaves
in Luxembourg Gardens, forgets the rose
of revolution, the pattern of lost graves.
The clever land-locked European follows
his routine in luxurious goodness
and wishes nothing but that those white rows
of stone should never soften his eyes' hardness.
He only desires words like 'buy' and 'sell'
and any others are unnecessary burdens.
Hence, even monosyllables like 'hell'
are skins to be sloughed off – with 'Jew', with 'war'.
He runs his business empire very well
and knows what he will do. He walks his whore
up to a laurel wreath on a red front door.

13                                    *FINLAND*

Up to a laurel wreath on a red front door
the children try their voices. The forest looms
about the house at Järvenpää and hums
*Tapiola.* The children are unsure
if this is right. What have they come here for?
But from the headland of far distant rooms
a sound like the wild geese's wing-beat booms.
It is the master. Ready with the choir ...
And do not ask him why there is no Eighth
or why, in thirty years, he has not composed
a tune to equal this. He is not to blame
for how the spirits treat him. It is late
to wish for pearls, those lips have been long closed,
though children know things cannot stay the same.


14                                    *IRELAND*

Though children know things cannot stay the same,
their border-country parents try to keep
whatever's precious to them – keep the blame,
the bigotry, the bombs, maintain the cheap
hypocrisy that's served them well, the deep
commitment to intransigence and a pure
religious sentiment that will endure
as long as wolves still like the look of sheep.
They teach their children to obey the call
of lights there on the peace-line – orange, green,
(but never red) – to cheer the truth of lies,
to spray (but never read) the writing on the wall,
yet not think what's beyond, not think how when
a wall is breached, the water levels rise.

15                          *UNITED KINGDOM*

A wall is breached, the water levels rise,
old pasturelands abandoned to the sea:
slow hissing submission of industry ...
Tsunamis conquer and then colonise
the peace, burying storm-force under beaches.
Whatever crowns were once displayed have gone
on an air tour, their only jewel the sun
to carry, on a fair-day cure. With butchers,
circling a calm denial of mass graves,
ask what that pride they boasted of was for –
these few cold peaks, a lyric verse, a name?
All dream of warmth, youth, kicking through dry leaves
up to a laurel wreath on a red front door,
though children know things cannot stay the same.

# BONE MUSIC

## (1998–2009)

*So little cause for carolings*
*Of such ecstatic sound …*
                        Hardy

## OLD SHUCK

where the cloudscape is a parade of vapour trails and blue ideas
where the horizon fizzes to its power lines of poplar and spire
where the windmills prop themselves like armless Puritan soldiers
where the church quivers as a bog oak heaves from the grave
where the ditches lure young drivers with their murky pheromones
where the peat shrinks from silver tracks as they press their advance

*the black dog sits*

## FEN FRIENDS
*for my daughter at twelve*

Do they hear the punt-guns' ghostly echo in the small hours,
feel the jelly under their feet as they blow out their birthdays,
dream of the Black Dog? Or imagine they glimpse their reflections
beckon through the silvering of a dust-storm over Soham.

## PERIGEE AT CHRISTMAS

The moon is as close tonight as it ever comes:
a miner's lamp, it drills out sleighbells from our rooms.

But we are as far from Christmas as it is possible to get.
That star in the east is the video recorder set

to capture all the other star appearances of the holiday.
Only the cat seems able to rewind herself automatically

from the smell of the kitbit stocking she has been given.
If I could find a stable, I would be dreaming of a heaven

where there are no cotton-wool deceits to perpetrate
and parents do not have to sit up into the small hours, waiting

for children to drop their guard (their greed) so that the myth
kitty can be fed: a place where peace on earth

includes a full night's sleep each Christmas Eve
(as much a right as magic in childhood) and a reprieve

from this wind that's like the spirit's battery of a day
moonlight will abandon to electronic goods and play.


## BONES

*Play the bones*

when the news comes on
and a voice intones
the lists of the dead

*Play the bones*

when electric chairs
are restored as thrones
for a shaven head

*Play the bones*

when a lump appears
and the doctor phones
but there's still no bed

*Play the bones*

when the missiles chew
on those foreign loans
that were meant for bread

*Play the bones*

when the kids on line
turn to making clones
in the garden shed

*Play the bones*

when the battles start
in tourist zones
other trade has fled

*Play the bones*

when a driver fails
to observe the cones
on the months ahead

*Play the bones*

when the years stoop
to pick up stones
for some words you said

## July 12th
*for Evelyn Glennie*

Protestantism beats the air polyrhythmical,
crowds press to the barriers at Drumcree.

While here in a middle England chapel, we file
to occupy all sides of a loaded stage.

Bombs home-made from treaties soaked in hatred
burn the Garvaghy Road. We look at an oil-drum

or turn a discreet page. The RUC get out
their riot shields, the troops load rubber bullets.

We prepare our applause, a tam-tam waiting
to swell, a secular gamelan. Black hats

attend to the Grand Master of the Orange Order.
We – to a loose gown and hair, bare feet.

Peace is forgotten, all palms are closed to it.
But she picks up two sticks and begins a new

piece called *Darkness to Light*, frightening a child
in the front row, who has to be carried out,

but exploding into the dance-floor colours of this
converted nave a wave to thrill those of us

perched nervously on the edge. In Ulster
this night three children are set on fire

in a sectarian arson attack. Darkness to
light, the marimba reminds us, glowing its

optimism against the death rattle and attack of
drumkit, Drumcree and deafening Lambeg drums.

## Aisling

We sway,
dark, unrecorded
and beautiful
like bard song
on the air
or like
a selection
of lutes to play
your galliards on.

Our unborn
capering in us
to the rope's jig
at Smerwick –
you, and Grey
and Edmund Spenser
appreciate the dying
fall of
the Irish mothers.

Our lovers
you have taken
to be a consort
of viols and drawn
their guts before
the Fairy
Queen of English
to glib-eyed
silence.

Our language
is mere howling
beyond the pale
wherein
a forty-part
motet of women's
voices plays –
four hundred years
in the unravelling.

## OFFICERS OF THE 198TH BATTERY

Was there really a Sergeant-Major Death
    in Grandpa's artillery regiment?
    Here's the name, falling in at the end
of a list of the Hundred and Ninety-Eighth

Battery's officers, marching in smooth,
    unironic, steady, cursive hand
    from General to Colonel to Adjutant
with nothing (except perhaps the faint wraith

of a recoil about its blue-black path)
    to make it more than just a name like Lieutenant
    Choked-on-mustard-gas or Captain Blown-into-
next-century. It has my grandfather's

brand of humour – branding the shed he bequeathed
    *The Better 'Ole* like a postcard from the Front,
    or sticking his scraped-out pipe-bowl under
my young nose so I have to fight to breathe.

## OTTO HAHN IN HUNTINGDONSHIRE

Six miles a day he walked, around and around
that walled garden, fifty times, and for each
rotation a cipher chalked on the wall.

But even after he had left, the number
of scratches on its pale skin would be tiny
compared with the children's shadows etched

into that other ground. He had always sworn
if Hitler cracked the secret of the A-bomb,
he would kill himself. And now this officer

approaches with the news that the Nobel Prize
research into bombardment of uranium
he led has led tonight to Hiroshima.

Nine physicists are amused at such blatant
propaganda, but Hahn stops walking, his face
black, his mind on its one track, flowering

maths, deaths, *Metamorphosen,* as he gouges
his initials, O H, again and again
in the warm August brickwork of Farm Hall.

The angelic voice in the British uniform
is asking why he's so upset – *after all,*
*better a few thousand Japs than one single ...*

Hahn's O splits open before his eyes,
a cock's egg that he fantasised has hatched,
Godmanchester cracks, and the Ouse comes slithering.


## Enigma Variations

He takes a bite out of the poisoned apple
and falls into oblivion. At your computer
you google Alan Turing: the green secret
begins its paring, red Englishness decoded
as he and others closeted in Bletchley
succeed in cracking Germany's Enigma.

But who will colour in this blank enigma?
Of those who were the first to taste the apple
among ten thousand pigeon-holed at Bletchley,
none knew they were inventing the computer,
none guessed they were a key to be decoded
themselves, perhaps a better feathered secret

than anything the Wrens sat on (*Top Secret*),
who now nest in a petrified Enigma
Machine of history's making, undecoded,
unable to confess they'd eaten apple,
(the green, the red) except to their computer
or, sixty years on, flitting out to Bletchley

from caves where no wall ever echoed 'Bletchley',
to let the children know we know their secret,
that here we summoned it – some new computer
adventure they're addicted to: *Enigma*,
*Colossus* or *Station X*. An apple
whose bite has turned Socratic and, decoded,

spells Alan Turing. So much to be decoded,
refreshed, acknowledged. Here at sunny Bletchley
Park fruit is swelling. Tree takes back its apple,
admits paternity, blurts out the secret
pollinating power-buzz of Enigma,
its bombes, ripe, orotund. In each computer

hard-drive are pigtails, plaits, a young computer
rooting for its terminal, the drum-encoded
dream of at last deciphering enigmá-
tic whirring from hacked hedgerows even Bletchley
ignored: the core, the pre- and post-war secret
unsolved since birds first pecked the human apple.

An apple fell beneath Hut 8 at Bletchley,
its seed not yet decoded; a computer
receives its secret mating call: *enigma.*

## To A Blitz Survivor

Pulled out from under the rubble of stories,
mother of pearl, ivory, gut and plaster,
where a stairway uncoils, hissing, and a door
is opening on to the Blackout: a cast,
a props list, suburban dramatics, crammed
into a sealed chimney's priest-hole in your post-
holocaust living room. The doodlebugs hum
down in the skirting. What is it you most

remember about the Blitz? That split-
silence before a V2? Or were they for you
'the best years of your life'? Beethoven's Fate
hammering at the felt, and passing through
into a dusty morning-after, all memory
cleared, the East End like a pub piano
with missing keys, but in the National Gallery
Hess plays on? It's only today we view,

engraved beneath the kitchen table where you slept,
those nights the sky fell in; or overturn
the mask you would not wear; or hear a dropped
chance remark, myths unexploded that were
nothing at the time. Stuka and Incendiary,
your dome has survived. You did not burn,
but married, trying to forget how you had spent
six years in labour, for us to be born.

## TRIBUTE

At Fotheringhay, she's
thrown a swan's feather
into the Nene,
not to say 'coward',

not for those mute
numbers migrating
and breeding in Iraqi
airspace, but as her

tribute (like this
wreath here, freshly
laid, its ballpoint
message targeting

'murder') to the one
fragment that would not
be moved by a bullying
dynasty. It is still

February. The river,
however, is king
of spin and makes
my daughter's offering

an accusation, turning
a hunched back
away from us and
on to March

to advance in ruled
straight lines
towards the empire
of the Wash, her feather's

opinion, like her father's,
caught by the downing
thistlebeds and banks
of oil-stained bush.

*21st February 2003*

## MENE MENE

The bomber wrote its message above Baghdad
and from its shadow something dark slipped
to explode in a cluster of clay tablets,
figurines, seals, pottery, tools.

The target, a secret arms factory,
was intact, but all around were bursting
friezes and faces, a ram from a thicket,
a gold harp, a dagger, a chariot

and coins, coins ... Carefully guided
mythology from the third millennium before
Christ, lovingly crafted smart
technology from Ur, the war-games of Gil-

gamesh played by all those generals
in cuneiform in the history bunker, like Dudu
of Lagash, or Shalmaneser, or Belshazzar
safe behind the wall of Babylon HQ.

## SEATTLE

Bezelled, faceted ridge –
like a printout at the foot
of a hospital bed.

Seattle cannot see it,
he is laid out
with a hopelessly broken tribe.

White men come around
with their accoutrements
and their potlatch: we

will be transferring you
to a more convenient place
afterwards, they say,

they need his bed,
they need his agreement,
the name of his next of kin,

offering a quiver of pills
and a tube to breathe
peace through, peace,

removing the oxygen tepee,
the totem drip, masked
for the scalp dance.

## OXYGEN

Discussing the Continuous Positive Airway
Pressure device as news comes
of a Helios Airways catastrophic cabin
pressure failure suffocating the crew
and all passengers. Their deaths inter-
rupt my sleep now more than any snoring:

a marble frieze of children's faces
with bunched masks hanging as the dark
frost dreams them into a peak near Athens.

Waking, I remember Uncle Georg
who owned the Sandmann vineyard, ripening
slowly beneath his survival tent,
steeped in its clear wine, breathing
its anti-freeze, until he is empty
of everything but emphysema. I am in love

with your breathing and with being here
on earth with you who were born to the gasp
and clink of bottles and the news from Everest.

## THE HEALING

*London, 8th June 2007*                    *with Rosie and Jane*

Where John Lill tells us how he became John ill
so no one turned up for the concert, the remains of London Wall
obtrude among the flats; and a steely girls' school
echoes Lady Eleanor Holles' footsteps to the roll-call
of fire, Great Fire and Blitz. Twice, nothing was left
but the tower, some walls, a name – St Giles, Cripplegate –
like a smouldering miraculous exposition repeat.
Shakespeare's development. Cromwell's marriage. Milton laid
to rest in its uncanny peace: the perfect recording venue.
Speed and Frobisher memorialised on the walls, two
who could have been our guides through the mirror-maze of new
worlds round the Barbican, past Moorfields, out of Bedlam to
the Stairs of Life and the Ward of St Giles Without:
a broken, dream-like place. Now, raised by Moonlight,
by Preludes in B minor, G sharp minor and by the flitting
minor masterpieces dear to the Lloyd Webbers' late
neglected father, my daughter and her boyfriend are quietly
rapt, the bust of Milton, bomb-shaken, mutely
unimpressed by the presence in the back pew of a celebrity,
but hearing Paradise, as I am, gradually, gratefully.

*Manchester, 9th June 2007*                    *with my mother*

Schumann threw himself in the Rhine, and now
it rises by capillary action through
the strings and horns, a cathedral sound
no morning-after pattern of the Allies'
mercy could rival. This stinging in the eyes
is Kölnisch Wasser the music draws
out of an old canal in Manchester
where youngsters singing from the pub stagger
across a lock gate. Behind the Bridgewater,
a song-line from the Rhenish Symphony arched
over the barging menace of the dark
still glows and points to where our gold is parked.

*Oxford, 17th June 2007*                    *with Katie*

For healing, you'd prescribed the Holywell:
the Dante String Quartet to escort me down
and back to Papa's pure C major. By chance
(the chance that makes me turn a page and find
emotion's limits, the music beyond
the notes, within the unmoved stone of things),
we are not in the Holywell at all,
but Mary Magdalene's domain: Maudlin,
where Haydn's dry sticks have been whirled to blazes
by Tchaikovsky's love circle. Outside the hall,
I talk with your friend Dragon, not about
the music, but of building in stone, St Paul's,
the Fire, Wren's flight. Architecture as the egg
we hoard, a huge blown shell in the drawer marked
'Things to Keep'. Then, since it's Father's Day,
we've climbed Headington Hill. And only now
I see the cranes stir over lab and mosque
with their new dreams, and note the empty stave
the pylons keep across the Cumnor hills
as grey threatens, do I recall 'the spark
from heaven', do I feel the healing start.

## SWEET VALE OF AVOCA

My daughter is singing
at the Meeting of the Waters.

She is wearing the green
coat I have criticized

for its impractical
embroidery, its dragon

coiled ineffectually
against the cold.

An old fisherman
is standing by his line

like a man who does not
exist as one stream

passes into another
and there is a brief

glittering quarrel
around nothing.

But it is warm here
in the October sun

as her voice rises
in its scales, leaping

from 'bright waters'
to 'the last rays'.

## OUROBOROS

Some islands are no more than those we see
on summer evenings – clouds beyond the glass
that shape archipelagoes of light, and gloss
our storm-beaten dreams. Others feel wintry
and real – have motorbikes, are sanctuary
to dogma, gull, anthrax; a royal house;
Thelwell's ponies; or Muir's heraldic horse ...
Though John Donne rings in our ears at the ferry
and bridge, tolling the mainland, still our need
for solitude keeps pressing here where crowds
are pasted up against shopfronts while cars
tourney and quest for space. The errant creed
is 'we move on'. But on islands, all roads
return to meet themselves, their one route ours.

## WINTERREISE
*Fitzwilliam College, Cambridge*

The Eurovision Song Contest tonight –
the nation nails itself to plasma screens.
But we have climbed the stiles and walked the flats
and sharps of an arterial path, where fens
whistle us (mill stream, linden, lantern-light
or crow), following Schubert's finger signs,
to hear a young man sinking to the height
of his powers, while the organ-grinder grinds.

## ROSIE ON THE ROAD TO PRAGUE

It's minus one here
and minus much more
in Wenceslas Square
where snow lies deep
and even the drip
of her texts in our sleep
makes an icicle.
The piteous call
of St Nicholas' bell
across the frontiers
is nowhere so fierce
or lovely as hers.

## PELLEGRINI STAIRCASE
*Kimbolton Castle*

As she ascended,
a minstrel leant

down to pet a small
dog, and a monkey

shifted towards a
trompe l'œil cherub.

Halfway up, she met
Caesar staring out

from his chariot
across the bustle

of pigments and brush
strokes; and as she

reached the top, she
turned to see the whole

procession shimmer into
life, its sunlight

unfrozen by a slow
allegorical motion

southwards that leaves
only bare Augustan

whitewash billowing
after the triumph that was

Venice, the walls
reflecting each other

like heroic couplets
searching for a rhyme.

## DEATHS IN VENICE

I

A horn call over the lagoon: he's dead,
the carnival's masked hero, darkest knight
in all its glittering shallows. Wagner's deathbed
accompaniment – his 'Farewell' – was a bright
and cheerful *gondolieri* tune. His head
dropped forward, pocket watch slipped out of sight
and stopped, the grail is lost and music floats
to its funeral. Twelve oars. A row of notes.

II

Another blast. Another slow cortège
from *Ca' Rezzonico* now, the home of Pen
whose ink has run so low his father's page
is blank, for all those years of love and lend.
Fame throws its rope towards the landing stage
and misses, falls into the bluey green
oblivion of the Grand Canal, as Robert Browning
departs and leaves his dry son drowning.

III

Dim land. Peace. Then a brassy broadcast sound
between the gondolas; invisible waves
breaking over stages, unsettling ground
whose very foundations rot. Literature heaves
its driftwood, bringing with it Ezra Pound
to cemetery island. A storm raves
and seaweed scribbles free verse in the sand;
the Lido goes on listening to its oompah band.

IV

No sound when they lay down Diaghilev
or when Stravinsky joined him for that one
last dance through time, beyond belief
and into myth. Watched by the evening sun
behind the city, from their spotlit grave
they count the dreadful complex beats that soon
will tell them: your scene's over. But the rite
they share this time is one long opening night.

## AFTER THE MAHLER

After the *Symphony of a Thousand*
I am woken by the solitary
figure of my father walking

along a lonely road, just as
he was before he died.
I shout to stop the car,

leap out and embrace him
feeling the stubble and warmth
of his presence. Where we were

going, where the road
was winding to in my dream
I do not know. But years ago

we reeled out of a Prom,
where I had been standing
in the arena and he was sitting

somewhere up in the gods,
to meet at the bus-stop and rejoice
in what we had heard:

*Veni Creator Spiritus ...*
*Blicket Auf ...* as Faust
is raised to the empyrean.

## VARIATIONS ON A GHAZAL

What is music? A sculpture carved out of air.
A counterpoint of earth, water, fire in the air.

It eats into the barnacled hull of work and pay,
drawing out its gold-fingered wire from the air.

Collar and veil and cocoon of a flame that converts
touchpaper lives to its pyre. It's the air

that the clay on bootsoles wishes for when it urges
our feet more slowly, much higher, where the air

is only fit for spheres. Music is the seed
within such bubble inspirations that aspire on the air,

then burst into canopy. It is a figured fermenting
in our cellars, the progress of Gaia through the air

to demijohn, a greening of black ashbuds, when all
sobriety and sackcloth vows expire to the air.

## VIENNA
*in memory of HK*

'When I worked for Hans Keller'
sounds – I don't know ...
                    Vienna
is waiting.
          My daughter
sang Billy Joel
from the piano, then off to Munich,
Berchtesgaden, Dachau.

Now it's our turn. The waltz
begins, La Ronde, the Ring-
strasse whirling us past
the Opera and Mahler and Strauss's
syrupy pool where a heart
should be ...
    something Hans
once said, as he said
he didn't believe in the infinitely
postponed concentration
made possible by capturing
sounds: 'unmusic', unmoving.

His testimony resounds
in spite of bytes, laser,
diamond, recording head
or thorn.
    The morning after
Kristallnacht: *Since when
have you been a homosexual?
How many Aryan girls
have you seduced?* 'The various
types of beating'. The chase
down corridors between
the staves of SS
rifle-butts.

    (Who's riding
so late through darkening wind
past the Schubert Garage
where the Erlking's eyes
leer out from a Volkswagen Beetle
to the birthplace and the glasses
under glass?)

    After three days,
food. After four, someone
screams and is shot. Another
jumps from the fourth floor.

In Haydngasse, baroque
and biedermeier for his work

on 'The Creation', I decline
the 'Chaos' button, choose
a charming minuet
while I look at the death mask,
beating: *two, three …*

They are ordered to face the wall.

When I worked for Hans,
he gave me his book, inscribed
'by way of functional welcome'.

If they move, they will be shot.

The book describes his escape
from Vienna
                from the heart
                          un-
moving for three hours

the home
                where Mozart loved
his billiard table, Constanze
and 'Figaro'
               unmoving
for four hours
                  and the six
quartets for Papa Haydn
who heard in G major
the future of music.
                *Tomorrow*
*at six you will be castrated,*
*at eight you will be executed.*

Vienna, where Hans resolved
if he ever got free
he would never again be in
a bad mood.

                Freud's
spark from the gods is a slice
of Sachertorte.

*Why are you*
*bleeding all over? Oh, well,*
*I fell down a flight of stairs.*
*Did anybody beat you? No.*
*Did you see anybody beating*
*anybody? No.*

The steps
climb to the fourth floor
to the room where Beethoven heard
nothing.

I remember Hans
explaining how the best introductions
occur in the middle – witness
opus one hundred and thirty –

but which way to choose
for a finale?

Chased down
passages of a Great Fugue
which finishes as he crashes
into a glass door and smashes
through it out on to the street?

Or the witty moto perpetuo
of critical neurones dancing?

## SULIS MINERVA IN STONELY

You would not know there was an ancient well
behind this forsythia, until it rains
and then you hear that hollow passing-bell
tolling a pure life laid down for the mains,

reminding you of rabbits loosely slung
within its cool, damp lip by the gamekeeper,
of that old woman someone told you flung
herself into its gullet. The well is deeper

than common sense might think: down sixteen feet,
past snail and weed and slime, the plumb-bob rests
on things you cannot know. The only date
it utters is a zero, the only guests

it sings of are those who in passing fed
a coin, a bell, a jewel down its throat
or – earlier still – a skull, a severed head.
Its one response, that grateful bottom note.

# MOSAIC
*for Jane*

Aswan, Arbroath –
our lives have marked the limits
of an Empire

you would always take
the Roman roads. *Look! the agger! And here's*
*where the Fosse Way crosses …*
                              or you'd be off
alone out over the moor at Blackstone Edge
to see, to walk, via some warp in time,
the paved stone street

| on either side | the traffic passing | to counterthrust |
| of an arch | through it, 'all | and the keystone |
| that never sleeps, | experience', thrust | still unmoved |

At Bignor, at Fishbourne, we bought the same English Heritage mugs
with images of gods copied from the floors of colonial dining rooms.

But now they are plain white, plunged into nothingness like burial urns.

across
            our meandering
                        East Anglian
                                    homeward
                                                stroll
the local dowser feels
                        the twilight being cut
                                                by a sharp

                                    profile
                        the shadow
            of another road
advancing


I think of the footsoldiers
in York

                        where you and I
                        in a silvery post-
                        coitus lay thigh
                        against thigh

                                                the footsoldiers
                                                in the Treasurer's House
                                                walking
                                                dejectedly
                                                cut off at the knees
                                                disappearing into a wall


            pre-nuptial seconds climbing Maiden Castle ·
            childless minutes counting down to Constantine ·
            hours at play with potsherds, beads and middens ·
            days in the educational leadmines · weeks and months
            road-laying, fort-building, fighting · only Chedworth
            in a lifetime of villas offering solace · domestic
            perfection · the bath-house · the hypocaust · the four seasons
            mosaic · undeclining because there is no autumn

in Stanwick, where pianist
and oboist live
Vivaldi calls above

the voices on the air
*I'll be there shortly*
*I'm on my way*

while Orpheus plays
for his lost love
beneath the set-aside.

a
clay
Venus
from
one
of
three
Godmanchester
temples
it  is
a  fit
offering

Milecastle, turret, turret – everywhere searching for the Vallum.
Accepting a lift from a strange old man with an owl.

Minerva, Mithras, the incessant pagan rain, a ghost
at every crossroads, a lost legion, an inscription in the mist.

The same rain ensuring Coventina's well is filled,
that floods the Matres, the phallus stone. We conceive our child.

# INDEX AND BIOGRAPHICAL NOTE

# INDEX OF TITLES

Volumes in which poems first appeared are indicated in brackets:

BS – *The Bocase Stone* (1996), CP – *The Coastal Path* (1996),
F – *Fotheringhay* (1995), GE – *Gascoigne's Egg* (2000),
HK – *The Home Key* (2003), NF – *Nightflights* (1998),
OS – *Omm Sety* (2001), TV – *The Tutankhamun Variations*, (1991),
W – *Westerners* (1982), WJ – *Winter Journeys* (1984)

# BIOGRAPHICAL NOTE

JOHN GREENING was born in 1954 in Chiswick and was brought up in Hounslow, directly under the main flight path to Heathrow. He studied at the Universities of Swansea, Mannheim and Exeter and worked for a time as a children's magician before joining BBC Radio 3, where he was clerk to Hans Keller. His first mature poems were published in Emma Tennant's legendary 70s magazine, *Bananas* and he received much encouragement at this time from Ted Hughes. A two year spell with VSO in Egypt – where he was awarded the Alexandria Poetry Prize by Mrs Sadat – spawned his first book, *Westerners* (1982), and started an abiding obsession with all things Egyptian. He was given a Scottish Arts Council Award in the 1980s and, recently, an Authors' Foundation travel grant, but has generally made a living by teaching – for many years at Kimbolton School, but also in Upper Egypt, Scotland and the USA. He has been a poetry reviewer for the TLS since the 1990s and last year was asked to judge the Eric Gregory Awards. Amongst other prizes, he has won the Bridport (1998) and the TLS Centenary (2001). He received a Cholmondeley Award from the Society of Authors in June 2008, when his eleventh collection, *Iceland Spar*, also appeared. He has produced studies of the First World War Poets, W.B.Yeats, Ted Hughes, Thomas Hardy and Edward Thomas (all for Greenwich Exchange) and is currently editing an anthology of music poetry. His Niagara Falls song-cycle (to music by Paul Mottram) was premiered by the Dunedin Consort at the Wigmore Hall and toured Canada. His verse play about the Lindbergh kidnapping was performed in Asheville, North Carolina, in June 2002. He has contributed to several BBC radio programmes and to a television documentary about Dylan Thomas and Vernon Watkins. He has also lectured on Watkins (in Swansea), on the war poets (at the 2005 Ledbury festival) and gave the 2001 Jon Silkin lecture. He is well known as a creative writing tutor: for a decade at the Camelford Indian King Arts Centre and recently for the Poetry School in Cambridge. Married, with two daughters, John Greening still lives in the little game-keeper's cottage in Stonely, Huntingdonshire, where most of these poems were written.